Understanding Machine Learning: Build AI Models with Python

A Step-by-Step Guide to Developing Machine Learning Algorithms

BOOZMAN RICHARD

BOOKER BLUNT

Table of Content

TABLE OF CONTENTS

INTRODUCTION

Understanding Machine Learning: Build AI Models with Python

In the rapidly evolving world of technology, machine learning (ML) and artificial intelligence (AI) are no longer just buzzwords—they are the driving forces behind some of the most innovative and impactful advancements in various industries. From self-driving cars to personalized healthcare, ML models are reshaping how we approach problem-solving, decision-making, and automation. As these technologies continue to evolve, the need for professionals with a solid understanding of machine learning has never been greater.

Understanding Machine Learning: Build AI Models with Python is designed to guide you on your journey to mastering the fundamental and advanced concepts of machine learning. Whether you are a beginner looking to dive into the world of AI or an experienced practitioner seeking to refine your skills, this book offers clear explanations, practical examples, and hands-on projects to help you build and deploy machine learning models.

Why This Book?

Machine learning can often seem like a complex and intimidating field, with a multitude of algorithms, frameworks, and tools to master. However, this book breaks down the essentials of machine learning into approachable, easy-to-understand sections. Using Python—the most popular programming language for data science and machine learning—this book provides you with the skills you need to develop real-world machine learning models and understand the theoretical concepts behind them.

From the foundational techniques of supervised and unsupervised learning to cutting-edge applications of deep learning and natural language processing, this book offers a comprehensive approach to learning machine learning. Each chapter provides step-by-step instructions on building models, evaluating their performance, and deploying them in real-world applications.

What You Will Learn

1. **Foundational Concepts**: The book starts with an introduction to machine learning, explaining the core principles, types of learning (supervised,

unsupervised, reinforcement learning), and how data plays a critical role in developing successful models.

2. **Data Preprocessing**: One of the most critical aspects of machine learning is working with data. In the early chapters, you'll learn how to clean, transform, and scale data, handle missing values, and prepare your data for training models.

3. **Core Machine Learning Algorithms**: This book delves into the most widely used algorithms for regression, classification, clustering, and more. Whether it's linear regression, decision trees, or k-means clustering, you'll learn how to implement and optimize these models in Python.

4. **Deep Learning**: As the field of machine learning increasingly moves toward deep learning, we'll explore neural networks, convolutional neural networks (CNNs), and recurrent neural networks (RNNs), along with how to use frameworks like TensorFlow and Keras for building deep learning models.

5. **Model Evaluation and Tuning**: Understanding how well your model is performing is just as important as building it. This book covers techniques for evaluating models using metrics such as accuracy,

precision, recall, and F1 score. You'll also learn about hyperparameter tuning and methods to improve model performance.

6. **Real-World Applications**: Machine learning is not just an academic exercise—it has real-world applications across various industries. The book covers applications in fields like healthcare (disease prediction), finance (fraud detection), retail (recommendation systems), and more.

7. **Ethical Considerations and Challenges**: The growing use of AI raises important ethical questions. This book explores the challenges of ensuring fairness, reducing bias, and making machine learning models explainable and transparent.

8. **Deployment and Scaling**: Finally, the book walks you through deploying machine learning models in production environments. You will learn how to set up APIs with Flask or Django and how to deploy models to the cloud, ensuring that they are scalable and accessible for real-time predictions.

Practical Approach

This book emphasizes a **hands-on approach** to learning, meaning you'll spend more time building and testing machine learning models than just reading theory. Each chapter features practical examples and exercises that you can run on your own machine using Python and popular machine learning libraries like **Scikit-learn**, **TensorFlow**, and **Keras**. By the end of the book, you will have built several real-world machine learning applications, gaining valuable skills that can be directly applied in industry.

Who This Book is For

- **Beginners**: If you are new to machine learning or programming, this book will provide you with a clear, guided path to mastering the subject. No prior knowledge of machine learning is required, but basic knowledge of Python programming will be helpful.

- **Intermediate Learners**: For those with some experience in data science or machine learning, this book provides a deep dive into more advanced topics like deep learning, reinforcement learning, and model deployment. You'll also learn how to refine your models to make them more efficient and accurate.

- **Practitioners and Developers**: For professionals looking to apply machine learning in their work, the book covers best practices for deploying models in real-world environments, making it a valuable resource for anyone working in AI, data science, or software development.

Why Python?

Python has become the go-to language for machine learning and data science because of its simplicity and the vast ecosystem of libraries and tools available for these tasks. Whether it's data manipulation with **Pandas**, numerical computations with **NumPy**, or deep learning with **TensorFlow** and **Keras**, Python makes it easy to build, train, and deploy machine learning models. Throughout this book, we use Python to implement models, ensuring that you gain practical skills that are directly applicable in the industry.

Conclusion

Machine learning is one of the most exciting and fast-evolving fields in technology today. With applications ranging from personalized recommendations to medical diagnostics, its potential to transform industries is vast. This book provides you with the knowledge and skills needed to not only understand machine learning but to implement it in real-world scenarios, helping you build AI models that have tangible, impactful results.

The journey into machine learning can be complex, but with this book as your guide, you'll find a structured, practical approach that will help you become proficient in one of the most valuable skills of the 21st century. By the end, you'll not only have a strong foundation in machine learning but also the confidence to create and deploy machine learning models in production.

Get ready to unlock the power of machine learning and AI and start your journey toward becoming an expert in this transformative field.

CHAPTER 1

INTRODUCTION TO MACHINE LEARNING

What is Machine Learning?

Machine Learning (ML) is a branch of artificial intelligence (AI) that allows computers to learn from data without being explicitly programmed. At its core, machine learning involves building algorithms that can detect patterns in data and use those patterns to make predictions or decisions. For example, machine learning algorithms can help recognize images, predict stock prices, or recommend products based on user behavior.

Unlike traditional programming, where you provide a set of rules and instructions, machine learning models learn from experience and improve over time. This ability to adapt and improve without human intervention is what makes machine learning so powerful.

Brief History of Machine Learning and AI

The concept of machine learning dates back to the mid-20th century, evolving alongside the development of artificial intelligence (AI). Some key milestones in the history of machine learning include:

- **1950s:** Alan Turing proposed the "Turing Test," a measure of a machine's ability to exhibit intelligent behavior indistinguishable from that of a human. This laid the groundwork for AI research.

- **1957:** The first neural network, the Perceptron, was developed by Frank Rosenblatt, marking an early attempt to simulate human learning in machines.

- **1960s-1970s:** Early AI research focused on symbolic reasoning and expert systems. However, the lack of sufficient computing power and data limited progress.

- **1980s:** The rise of more advanced algorithms, such as backpropagation for training neural networks, reignited interest in machine learning.

- **2000s-Present:** With the advent of big data, faster processing power, and more sophisticated algorithms, machine learning has experienced explosive growth, leading to breakthroughs in deep learning, natural language processing, and reinforcement learning.

Key Terms in Machine Learning

To understand machine learning, it's important to familiarize yourself with some key terms:

- **Model:** A mathematical representation of a problem learned from data. It's the end result of training an algorithm.

14

- **Algorithm:** A set of rules or steps used to solve a problem, especially in data analysis and machine learning.
- **Training Data:** The dataset used to train a machine learning model. This data helps the model learn patterns and relationships.
- **Features (or Variables):** The attributes or inputs used by the model to make predictions.
- **Labels (or Target Variable):** The outcome or result the model is trying to predict or classify.
- **Overfitting:** When a model learns the training data too well, including noise and outliers, leading to poor performance on new, unseen data.
- **Underfitting:** When a model is too simple and fails to capture the underlying patterns in the data, leading to poor performance even on training data.

Types of Machine Learning: Supervised, Unsupervised, Reinforcement Learning

Machine learning can be broadly categorized into three types based on the learning process and the kind of data used:

- **Supervised Learning:** In supervised learning, the model is trained on labeled data, meaning the input data comes with corresponding output labels. The goal is for the model to learn a mapping between the input and output so

15

that it can make accurate predictions on new, unseen data. Examples of supervised learning algorithms include:

- o Linear Regression (for regression tasks)
- o Logistic Regression (for classification tasks)
- o Decision Trees
- o Support Vector Machines (SVM)

Example: A supervised learning algorithm might be used to predict house prices based on features like square footage, number of rooms, and location.

- **Unsupervised Learning:** In unsupervised learning, the model is trained on data that does not have labeled outputs. The goal is to find hidden patterns or intrinsic structures in the data. Common unsupervised learning algorithms include:

  - o K-Means Clustering
  - o Hierarchical Clustering
  - o Principal Component Analysis (PCA)

Example: Unsupervised learning might be used for customer segmentation, grouping customers with similar purchasing behavior.

- **Reinforcement Learning:** In reinforcement learning, an agent learns to make decisions by interacting with an environment. The agent receives rewards or penalties based on its actions and uses that feedback to improve its performance. Reinforcement learning is often used in situations where sequential decision-making is required, such as robotics and game-playing.

Example: A reinforcement learning algorithm might be used to train a robot to navigate a maze, with positive rewards for reaching the goal and negative penalties for hitting walls.

The Role of Data in Machine Learning

Data is the foundation of machine learning. In fact, the quality and quantity of data directly influence the performance of a machine learning model. Here's why data is so important:

- **Training and Testing:** Machine learning models are trained on historical data (training data) to learn patterns, and their performance is evaluated on a separate set of data (testing data) to ensure they generalize well to unseen examples.
- **Feature Engineering:** Data must be processed and transformed into a format suitable for machine learning algorithms. This step, known as feature engineering, involves selecting relevant features, scaling values, and sometimes creating new features based on the existing ones.

- **Bias in Data:** Machine learning models are only as good as the data they are trained on. If the data is biased or incomplete, the model will likely make biased or incorrect predictions. Therefore, data collection, cleaning, and preprocessing are critical steps in building reliable models.

As the field of machine learning continues to evolve, more data will be required to train increasingly complex models, especially for tasks like deep learning and reinforcement learning.

This chapter provides an overview of the foundational concepts of machine learning, including its history, key terms, types, and the central role that data plays in developing successful models. In the following chapters, you will explore each of these areas in more detail, along with hands-on examples to deepen your understanding.

CHAPTER 2

SETTING UP YOUR
DEVELOPMENT ENVIRONMENT

Installing Python and Necessary Libraries

Before diving into machine learning, the first step is to set up your development environment. Python is the most popular language for machine learning, thanks to its simplicity and extensive support through libraries. Here's how you can install Python and the essential libraries needed for machine learning:

1. **Install Python:**
   - Visit the official Python website at https://www.python.org/downloads/ and download the latest stable version of Python.
   - Follow the installation prompts for your operating system (Windows, macOS, or Linux).
   - During installation, make sure to check the option **"Add Python to PATH"** to avoid configuration issues later.
2. **Install Anaconda (Optional but Recommended):**
   - Anaconda is a distribution that comes with Python and many important libraries already

installed. It simplifies package management and environment setup.

- o Download Anaconda from https://www.anaconda.com/products/individual and follow the installation steps.

- o Once Anaconda is installed, you can use the `conda` command to manage packages and environments efficiently.

3. **Install Necessary Libraries:** If you're using a standard Python installation (not Anaconda), you can install libraries using Python's package manager, **pip**. Open your terminal or command prompt and run the following commands:

```bash

pip install numpy pandas matplotlib scikit-learn tensorflow jupyter
```

These libraries are the cornerstone of machine learning development:

- o **NumPy**: For numerical computing and handling large arrays.
- o **Pandas**: For data manipulation and analysis.
- o **Matplotlib**: For data visualization.
- o **Scikit-learn**: For machine learning algorithms and utilities.

20

o **TensorFlow**: For deep learning models.

Introduction to Jupyter Notebooks and IDEs

A good development environment can significantly speed up your workflow. Jupyter Notebooks and Integrated Development Environments (IDEs) are two powerful tools that will help you write and test Python code.

1. **Jupyter Notebooks:**
   o Jupyter Notebooks are interactive documents that allow you to mix code, text, and visualizations. They are widely used in data science and machine learning due to their ease of use and integration with Python libraries.
   o To launch Jupyter Notebooks, open your terminal or Anaconda prompt and type:

```bash
```

```
jupyter notebook
```

   o This will open a browser window where you can create, edit, and run Python code interactively. It's perfect for testing small code snippets and visualizing your results immediately.
2. **Integrated Development Environments (IDEs):**

21

- o IDEs are tools that provide a complete environment for writing, testing, and debugging code. For machine learning, the most popular IDEs include:
    - **PyCharm**: A feature-rich IDE specifically designed for Python.
    - **VS Code**: A lightweight, fast IDE that supports Python with the necessary extensions.
    - **Spyder**: An IDE focused on scientific development, often used in combination with Anaconda.
- o IDEs generally provide better code completion, debugging tools, and project management compared to Jupyter Notebooks.

Overview of Key Python Libraries: NumPy, Pandas, Matplotlib, Scikit-learn, TensorFlow

Machine learning development relies heavily on specific Python libraries that provide the necessary tools for data manipulation, analysis, modeling, and evaluation. Here's a brief overview of the key libraries you'll be using in this book:

1. **NumPy:**
    - o **Purpose**: Numerical computations and array manipulations.

22

- o **Key Features**:
  - Provides support for large, multi-dimensional arrays and matrices.
  - Offers mathematical functions like mean, standard deviation, and linear algebra operations.
  - **Example**: Creating and manipulating arrays in NumPy.

```python
python

import numpy as np
arr = np.array([1, 2, 3, 4, 5])
print(np.mean(arr))   # Output: 3.0
```

2. **Pandas:**
   - o **Purpose**: Data manipulation and analysis, particularly for structured data.
   - o **Key Features**:
     - Provides DataFrames, which allow easy handling of tabular data.
     - Supports data filtering, merging, and handling missing values.
     - **Example**: Loading a dataset and exploring it with Pandas.

```python
python
```

```
import pandas as pd
data = pd.read_csv('data.csv')
print(data.head())    # Displays the
first 5 rows of the dataset
```

3. **Matplotlib:**

   o **Purpose**: Data visualization.

   o **Key Features**:

      ▪ Provides a flexible way to create a wide range of plots (e.g., line plots, bar charts, histograms).

      ▪ Used to visualize the relationships between variables in your dataset.

      ▪ **Example**: Plotting data with Matplotlib.

   python

   ```
   import matplotlib.pyplot as plt
   x = [1, 2, 3, 4, 5]
   y = [1, 4, 9, 16, 25]
   plt.plot(x, y)
   plt.show()
   ```

4. **Scikit-learn:**

   o **Purpose**: Machine learning algorithms and utilities.

   o **Key Features**:

- Provides a wide variety of tools for classification, regression, clustering, and dimensionality reduction.
- Contains functions for model evaluation (e.g., accuracy, precision, recall) and cross-validation.
- **Example**: Training a machine learning model with Scikit-learn.

```python
from sklearn.model_selection import train_test_split
from sklearn.linear_model import LogisticRegression
X_train, X_test, y_train, y_test = train_test_split(X,                    y, test_size=0.2)
model = LogisticRegression()
model.fit(X_train, y_train)
print(model.score(X_test, y_test))
```

5. **TensorFlow:**

   o **Purpose**: Deep learning and neural networks.

   o **Key Features**:

      - Provides a comprehensive ecosystem for building deep learning models.

- Supports GPU acceleration and deployment to cloud platforms.
- **Example**: Building a simple neural network in TensorFlow.

python

```
import tensorflow as tf
model = tf.keras.Sequential([
    tf.keras.layers.Dense(64,
activation='relu',
input_shape=(X_train.shape[1],)),
    tf.keras.layers.Dense(1,
activation='sigmoid')
])
model.compile(optimizer='adam',
loss='binary_crossentropy',
metrics=['accuracy'])
model.fit(X_train,           y_train,
epochs=10)
```

First Hands-on: Running a Simple Python Script

Now that your development environment is set up, it's time to run a simple Python script. This will help you get familiar with the Python syntax and how to execute Python code in Jupyter Notebooks or an IDE.

1. **Hello, World! Python Script:**

o   Open a Jupyter notebook or IDE and type the following code:

```python
print("Hello, World!")
```

o   When you run this script, Python will print "Hello, World!" to the screen, confirming that everything is working correctly.

2. **Basic Math Operations:**

o   Try some simple calculations in Python:

```python
x = 10
y = 5
print("Sum:", x + y)
print("Difference:", x - y)
print("Product:", x * y)
print("Quotient:", x / y)
```

3. **Using Libraries:**

o   Import the NumPy library and perform a basic operation:

```python
import numpy as np
```

```
arr = np.array([1, 2, 3, 4, 5])
print("Array:", arr)
print("Sum of Array:", np.sum(arr))
```

Once you've completed this hands-on activity, you'll be ready to begin working with more complex machine learning tasks, knowing that your environment is set up and your basic skills are in place.

This chapter provided all the steps needed to set up your development environment and gave you a taste of Python programming. In the next chapter, we'll dive deeper into data preprocessing, a crucial step in any machine learning project.

CHAPTER 3

DATA PREPROCESSING: THE FOUNDATION OF MACHINE LEARNING

The Importance of Clean Data

In machine learning, data is the foundation upon which algorithms are built. However, raw data often comes in an unstructured or inconsistent format that can lead to incorrect model predictions if not properly cleaned and processed. Data preprocessing is a crucial step to ensure that your model receives accurate, meaningful data to learn from.

Clean data helps in:

- **Improved Model Accuracy**: Models trained on clean, well-prepared data typically produce better results.
- **Faster Convergence**: A well-prepared dataset allows machine learning algorithms to learn faster and more effectively.
- **Reduced Complexity**: By eliminating irrelevant, missing, or noisy data, you help reduce model complexity, improving generalization.

Key Preprocessing Steps:

- **Handling Missing Data**: If your dataset contains missing values, machine learning models will struggle to make predictions. Common methods to handle missing data include filling missing values with the mean, median, or mode of the column or using techniques like interpolation.

- **Removing Duplicates**: Duplicated data can skew your results, so identifying and removing duplicates is essential.

- **Handling Outliers**: Outliers, or extreme values, can mislead models by giving them undue weight. Identifying and handling these outliers (e.g., by capping or removing them) helps in building more reliable models.

Understanding Data Formats: CSV, JSON, SQL

Data comes in many formats, and understanding how to handle different types is essential for effective preprocessing. Here's an overview of the most common data formats:

1. **CSV (Comma Separated Values):**
    o CSV files are one of the simplest ways to store tabular data. Each line in a CSV file represents a row, and each column is separated by a comma.

- o **Usage**: CSV is widely used for exporting and importing data in data analysis and machine learning.
- o **Python Example**: Reading a CSV file with Pandas.

```python
import pandas as pd
data = pd.read_csv('data.csv')
print(data.head())    # Display the
first 5 rows
```

2. **JSON (JavaScript Object Notation):**
   - o JSON is a lightweight data-interchange format that stores data as key-value pairs. It's often used for web APIs and data interchange between systems.
   - o **Usage**: JSON is frequently used in web applications for exchanging structured data.
   - o **Python Example**: Loading data from a JSON file.

```python
import json
with open('data.json') as file:
    data = json.load(file)
```

31

```
print(data)
```

3. **SQL (Structured Query Language):**
   - o SQL is a domain-specific language used for managing and querying relational databases. SQL databases like MySQL, PostgreSQL, and SQLite are commonly used to store structured data.
   - o **Usage**: SQL is ideal for dealing with large, relational datasets.
   - o **Python Example**: Querying data from an SQL database.

```python
import sqlite3
conn                           =
sqlite3.connect('database.db')
query = "SELECT * FROM table_name"
data     =    pd.read_sql_query(query,
conn)
print(data.head())
```

Each of these formats requires specific tools and techniques to load, preprocess, and clean the data, which are essential steps before applying machine learning models.

Data Cleaning: Handling Missing Values, Duplicates, Outliers

Effective data cleaning is essential for creating reliable machine learning models. Below are some techniques for handling common issues in data:

1. **Handling Missing Values:** Missing data is a common issue, especially in real-world datasets. The goal is to either fill in the missing values or remove the rows/columns that contain them.

    o **Methods to Handle Missing Values:**

    ▪ **Drop rows or columns**: If the missing data is minimal, simply remove the rows or columns.

    ```python
    data.dropna(axis=0,
    inplace=True)  # Drop rows with
    missing values
    ```

    ▪ **Impute missing data**: Replace missing values with the mean, median, or mode.

    ```python
    data.fillna(data.mean(),
    inplace=True)        #   Replace
    ```

33

```
missing values with the column
mean
```

- **Advanced Imputation**: You can also use advanced imputation techniques like K-Nearest Neighbors (KNN) to predict missing values.

2. **Removing Duplicates:** Duplicates can distort the results of machine learning algorithms by giving undue weight to the same data points.

   o **Removing Duplicates**:

   python

   ```
   data.drop_duplicates(inplace=True)
   # Removes duplicate rows
   ```

3. **Handling Outliers:** Outliers are values that deviate significantly from other observations. They can have a strong impact on your machine learning model's predictions.

   o **Identifying Outliers**: Use statistical methods like Z-scores or IQR (Interquartile Range) to detect outliers.

   python

   ```
   Q1 = data['column'].quantile(0.25)
   ```

34

```
Q3 = data['column'].quantile(0.75)
IQR = Q3 - Q1
lower_bound = Q1 - 1.5 * IQR
upper_bound = Q3 + 1.5 * IQR
data     =    data[(data['column']    >=
lower_bound)    &    (data['column']    <=
upper_bound)]    # Remove outliers
```

Feature Scaling and Normalization

Machine learning algorithms typically perform better when the features (input variables) are on a similar scale. Without scaling, models may give more importance to higher-valued features.

1. **Feature Scaling**:
   o **Standardization**: This process involves rescaling the data to have a mean of 0 and a standard deviation of 1.

   ```python
   from   sklearn.preprocessing   import
   StandardScaler
   scaler = StandardScaler()
   data_scaled                        =
   scaler.fit_transform(data)
   ```

   o **Normalization**: Scaling the data so that all feature values are between 0 and 1.

35

```python
from sklearn.preprocessing import
MinMaxScaler
scaler = MinMaxScaler()
data_normalized                =
scaler.fit_transform(data)
```

2. **Why Scaling Matters**: Scaling ensures that each feature contributes equally to the model's performance, preventing algorithms like gradient descent from being biased toward larger values.

One-Hot Encoding and Label Encoding

When working with categorical data, machine learning algorithms typically require the data to be in numerical form. One-hot encoding and label encoding are two popular methods to handle categorical variables.

1. **Label Encoding**: Label encoding converts each category into a unique integer value.

```python
from        sklearn.preprocessing      import
LabelEncoder
encoder = LabelEncoder()
```

36

```
data['category']                              =
encoder.fit_transform(data['category'])
```

2. **One-Hot Encoding**: One-hot encoding creates a binary column for each category and assigns a 1 or 0 to indicate whether an observation belongs to that category.

```python
data          =          pd.get_dummies(data,
columns=['category'])  # One-hot encode the
'category' column
```

3. **When to Use Which?**:
   - **Label Encoding** is suitable for ordinal data (categories with a natural order like "Low," "Medium," and "High").
   - **One-Hot Encoding** is better for nominal data (categories without a natural order like "Red," "Blue," and "Green").

Data preprocessing is the essential first step in any machine learning pipeline. In this chapter, you learned about the importance of clean data, different data formats, and various techniques for cleaning, scaling, and encoding data. Proper data preparation ensures that your machine learning models have a solid foundation, allowing them to perform accurately and efficiently on real-world tasks.

In the next chapter, we'll dive into **Exploratory Data Analysis (EDA),** where we will visualize and analyze the dataset to uncover hidden patterns and insights.

CHAPTER 4

EXPLORATORY DATA ANALYSIS (EDA)

Introduction to EDA and its Purpose

Exploratory Data Analysis (EDA) is a critical process in the data analysis pipeline. It involves analyzing datasets to summarize their main characteristics, identify patterns, spot anomalies, and understand the relationships between variables. EDA helps you gain insights into your data, guiding decisions on which machine learning algorithms to use and how to preprocess the data for modeling.

The main goals of EDA are:

- **Understand Data Distribution**: Gain insight into the distribution of values in your dataset.
- **Detect Outliers**: Identify unusual data points that may skew the model.
- **Spot Relationships Between Features**: Discover correlations or dependencies between variables.
- **Visualize the Data**: Create graphical representations of the data to make patterns easier to understand.

By performing EDA, you ensure that you're not just blindly feeding data into a machine learning model but are actively involved in shaping your model's understanding of the problem.

Visualizing Data with Pandas and Matplotlib

Data visualization is one of the most effective ways to understand the structure and patterns in your data. Pandas and Matplotlib, two of the most popular Python libraries, make it easy to create insightful visualizations.

1. **Using Pandas for Basic Plots**: Pandas provides an easy way to plot data directly from DataFrames using the `plot()` method. This method allows you to create line plots, bar charts, histograms, and scatter plots.

    Example: Line Plot

    ```python
    python

    import pandas as pd
    import matplotlib.pyplot as plt

    # Load dataset
    data = pd.read_csv('data.csv')

    # Plot a line chart for a specific column
    data['column_name'].plot(kind='line')
    plt.title('Line Plot of Column Name')
    ```

40

```
plt.xlabel('Index')
plt.ylabel('Value')
plt.show()
```

2. **Using Matplotlib for More Customizable Plots**: While Pandas offers basic plotting capabilities, Matplotlib provides more flexibility and control over plot styling. You can use Matplotlib to create detailed and customized plots, including histograms, box plots, and scatter plots.

    Example: Scatter Plot

```python
python

import matplotlib.pyplot as plt

# Scatter plot
plt.scatter(data['column1'],
data['column2'])
plt.title('Scatter  Plot  of  Column1  vs
Column2')
plt.xlabel('Column1')
plt.ylabel('Column2')
plt.show()
```

3. **Histograms and Box Plots**: Histograms are useful for showing the distribution of a single feature, while box plots provide a summary of a feature's distribution, including the median, quartiles, and potential outliers.

41

Example: Histogram

```python
python
```

```python
data['column_name'].hist(bins=20)
plt.title('Histogram of Column Name')
plt.xlabel('Value')
plt.ylabel('Frequency')
plt.show()
```

Example: Box Plot

```python
python
```

```python
data['column_name'].plot(kind='box')
plt.title('Box Plot of Column Name')
plt.show()
```

Using Correlation Matrices

A correlation matrix is a table that shows the correlation coefficients between many variables in a dataset. Correlation coefficients range from -1 to 1, where:

- **1** indicates a perfect positive relationship,
- **-1** indicates a perfect negative relationship,
- **0** indicates no linear relationship.

Correlation matrices help identify relationships between features, which can guide feature selection for machine learning models. In general, highly correlated features might be redundant and could be dropped, while weakly correlated or uncorrelated features may carry unique information.

Example: Creating a Correlation Matrix

```python
import seaborn as sns

# Compute the correlation matrix
corr = data.corr()

# Plot the correlation matrix using a heatmap
sns.heatmap(corr, annot=True, cmap='coolwarm', fmt='.2f')
plt.title('Correlation Matrix Heatmap')
plt.show()
```

The heatmap provides a visual representation of the correlation matrix, with colors representing the strength of the correlation. Strong positive correlations are shown in one color, and strong negative correlations are shown in another.

Identifying Patterns and Relationships in Data

EDA is primarily about identifying patterns and relationships between different variables in your dataset. Visualization plays a key role in uncovering these patterns, but statistical methods also come in handy. Below are some common techniques used to uncover relationships:

1. **Scatter Plots for Bivariate Relationships**: Scatter plots are one of the best ways to identify relationships between two numerical variables. A clear linear or non-linear pattern may emerge, helping to identify possible predictors for modeling.

   Example: Scatter Plot of Two Variables

   python

   ```python
   plt.scatter(data['feature1'],
   data['feature2'])
   plt.title('Scatter   Plot:   Feature1   vs
   Feature2')
   plt.xlabel('Feature1')
   plt.ylabel('Feature2')
   plt.show()
   ```

2. **Pair Plots**: Pair plots display scatter plots for every pair of features in a dataset, providing a quick visual insight into relationships. This is particularly helpful for exploring small datasets with a few features.

   Example: Pair Plot

   python

44

```
sns.pairplot(data[['feature1', 'feature2',
'feature3']])
plt.show()
```

3. **Categorical Data Relationships**: For categorical data, use bar charts or count plots to analyze the frequency of each category. If you have a numerical target, you can also use box plots or violin plots to explore how the target variable behaves with respect to categorical features.

Example: Count Plot for Categorical Data

```
python
```

```
sns.countplot(x='category_column',
data=data)
plt.title('Category Distribution')
plt.show()
```

Example: Box Plot for Categorical vs Numerical Data

```
python
```

```
sns.boxplot(x='category_column',
y='numerical_column', data=data)
plt.title('Box    Plot:    Categorical    vs
Numerical')
plt.show()
```

45

Statistical Summary of Data

A good first step in understanding your data is to generate summary statistics, which provide insight into the central tendencies and spread of your data.

1. **Descriptive Statistics**: Pandas has built-in functions to generate a statistical summary of numerical features in your dataset, including the mean, median, standard deviation, minimum, and maximum.

    Example: Statistical Summary

    ```python
    python

    summary = data.describe()
    print(summary)
    ```

    This summary gives you a quick overview of your data, allowing you to spot any discrepancies, extreme values, or unusual distributions that may require further investigation.

2. **Skewness and Kurtosis**:
    o **Skewness**: Measures the asymmetry of the distribution of a dataset. Positive skew indicates a longer right tail, while negative skew indicates a longer left tail.

o **Kurtosis**: Measures the "tailedness" of the distribution. High kurtosis indicates a heavy tail, while low kurtosis indicates a light tail.

Example: Calculating Skewness and Kurtosis

python

```
print(data['column_name'].skew())          #
Skewness
print(data['column_name'].kurt())          #
Kurtosis
```

Understanding these statistical measures helps in identifying the distribution of your data, guiding decisions on transformations like normalization or log transformations.

Exploratory Data Analysis (EDA) is an essential step in any data analysis pipeline. It helps you understand the structure of your data, visualize relationships, identify patterns, and prepare for more advanced modeling. By using techniques such as correlation matrices, scatter plots, and statistical summaries, you can uncover valuable insights that will guide your machine learning process.

47

In the next chapter, we will dive into **Supervised Learning**, where we will focus on algorithms for predicting outcomes based on labeled data.

CHAPTER 5

INTRODUCTION TO SUPERVISED LEARNING

What is Supervised Learning?

Supervised learning is one of the most common types of machine learning, where the model is trained using labeled data. In supervised learning, each training example consists of an input and a corresponding output (the label), and the model learns to map inputs to the correct outputs. The goal is for the model to make predictions based on this learned relationship, which can then be tested on unseen data.

For example, in a classification task, the input could be an image of a handwritten digit, and the output (label) would be the corresponding digit. The model learns to classify digits by being trained on a large dataset of labeled images. In a regression task, the input could be features like square footage, number of rooms, and location, and the output would be the price of the house.

Supervised learning can be further divided into two main types:

- **Classification**: The model predicts a categorical label (e.g., "spam" or "not spam").

49

- **Regression**: The model predicts a continuous value (e.g., predicting house prices).

Key Algorithms in Supervised Learning

Supervised learning algorithms are designed to solve classification and regression problems. Some of the most widely used algorithms include:

1. **Linear Regression** (for regression tasks):
   - A simple algorithm used to predict a continuous target variable based on one or more input features.
   - **Example**: Predicting the price of a house based on its size.
   - **Mathematical Model**: A straight line that best fits the data points in the dataset.

```python
from      sklearn.linear_model      import
LinearRegression
model = LinearRegression()
model.fit(X_train, y_train)
```

2. **Logistic Regression** (for classification tasks):
   - Despite its name, logistic regression is used for binary classification problems. It models the

probability that a given input belongs to a certain class.

- o **Example**: Classifying an email as "spam" or "not spam."

- o **Mathematical Model**: A logistic function that outputs a value between 0 and 1, interpreted as the probability of belonging to one class.

python

```
from        sklearn.linear_model        import
LogisticRegression
model = LogisticRegression()
model.fit(X_train, y_train)
```

3. **Decision Trees** (for both classification and regression):
   - o A decision tree splits the dataset into subsets based on feature values and assigns labels or predictions based on the majority class or average value in each subset.
   - o **Example**: Classifying whether a customer will buy a product based on age, income, and other features.

python

```
from        sklearn.tree        import
DecisionTreeClassifier
```

51

```
model = DecisionTreeClassifier()
model.fit(X_train, y_train)
```

4. **Random Forest** (for both classification and regression):
   - ○ A random forest is an ensemble method that combines multiple decision trees to improve performance and reduce overfitting.
   - ○ **Example**: Predicting whether a loan will be approved based on applicant features.

python

```
from        sklearn.ensemble        import
RandomForestClassifier
model = RandomForestClassifier()
model.fit(X_train, y_train)
```

5. **Support Vector Machines (SVM)** (for both classification and regression):
   - ○ SVMs work by finding a hyperplane that best separates the classes in the feature space. They can handle both linear and non-linear data through kernel tricks.
   - ○ **Example**: Classifying images of cats and dogs.

python

```
from sklearn.svm import SVC
model = SVC()
```

```
model.fit(X_train, y_train)
```

6. **K-Nearest Neighbors (KNN)** (for both classification and regression):

   o KNN is a simple algorithm that makes predictions based on the majority label of the "K" nearest data points.

   o **Example**: Classifying a new data point based on the class of its nearest neighbors.

```python
from        sklearn.neighbors        import
KNeighborsClassifier
model                                       =
KNeighborsClassifier(n_neighbors=3)
model.fit(X_train, y_train)
```

These algorithms are the backbone of supervised learning, and the choice of algorithm depends on the type of problem you are trying to solve (classification vs. regression) and the nature of your dataset.

Understanding Training and Testing Data

In supervised learning, the dataset is typically split into two parts:

53

- **Training Data**: This is the subset of the dataset used to train the machine learning model. The model learns patterns and relationships from the training data.
- **Testing Data**: This is the subset of the dataset that is not used during training but is used to evaluate the model's performance. The testing data helps you assess how well the model generalizes to new, unseen data.

A typical practice is to divide the dataset into 80% training data and 20% testing data. This can be done using the `train_test_split()` function in Scikit-learn:

```python
from sklearn.model_selection import train_test_split
X_train, X_test, y_train, y_test = train_test_split(X, y, test_size=0.2, random_state=42)
```

It's also common to use **cross-validation**, where the data is split into multiple subsets (folds), and the model is trained and tested multiple times on different combinations of these subsets to get a more reliable performance estimate.

Overfitting vs. Underfitting

In machine learning, overfitting and underfitting are common problems that affect the performance of the model.

- **Overfitting**: This occurs when the model learns the training data too well, capturing noise and outliers. As a result, the model performs well on the training data but poorly on unseen testing data. Overfitting typically happens when the model is too complex for the given data.
    - o **Solution**: Simplify the model, use regularization techniques, or collect more data.
- **Underfitting**: This happens when the model is too simple and cannot capture the underlying patterns in the data. It leads to poor performance on both the training and testing data.
    - o **Solution**: Increase the complexity of the model or add more relevant features.

The goal is to find the right balance between overfitting and underfitting, which is known as the **bias-variance tradeoff**. One way to mitigate both is by using techniques like cross-validation or regularization.

Performance Metrics: Accuracy, Precision, Recall, F1 Score

Performance metrics are used to evaluate how well a machine learning model is performing, especially when working with classification tasks. These metrics help you assess the model's strengths and weaknesses.

1. **Accuracy**:
    o   Accuracy is the simplest metric and measures the overall percentage of correct predictions made by the model.
    o   **Formula**:

    Accuracy=Number of Correct PredictionsTotal Number of Predictions\text{Accuracy} = \frac{\text{Number of Correct Predictions}}{\text{Total Number of Predictions}}Accuracy=Total Number of PredictionsNumber of Correct Predictions

    o   **Example**: In a binary classification task, if a model correctly predicts 80 out of 100 instances, its accuracy is 80%.

```python
from sklearn.metrics import accuracy_score
accuracy = accuracy_score(y_test, y_pred)
```

2. **Precision**:

- o Precision measures the proportion of positive predictions that are actually correct. It is especially important when false positives have serious consequences (e.g., spam detection).

- o **Formula**:

  Precision=True PositivesTrue Positives+False P ositives\text{Precision} = \frac{\text{True Positives}}{\text{True Positives} + \text{False Positives}}Precision=True Positives+False Posit ivesTrue Positives

- o **Example**: In a medical diagnosis scenario, precision would measure how many of the predicted positive diagnoses are truly correct.

```python
from         sklearn.metrics          import
precision_score
precision   =    precision_score(y_test,
y_pred)
```

3. **Recall** (Sensitivity or True Positive Rate):

- o Recall measures the proportion of actual positives that are correctly identified by the model. It's important when false negatives are critical (e.g., cancer detection).

- o **Formula**:

  Recall=True PositivesTrue Positives+False Neg atives\text{Recall} = \frac{\text{True Positives}}{\text{True Positives} + \text{False Negatives}}Recall=True Positives+False Negati vesTrue Positives

- o **Example**: In a fraud detection system, recall measures how many fraudulent transactions were correctly detected.

```python
from sklearn.metrics import recall_score
recall = recall_score(y_test, y_pred)
```

4. **F1 Score**:
   - o The F1 score is the harmonic mean of precision and recall, offering a balance between them. It's particularly useful when dealing with imbalanced datasets, where accuracy alone may not provide a true picture of the model's performance.
   - o **Formula**:

F1 Score=2×Precision×RecallPrecision+Recall\text{F1 Score} = 2 \times \frac{\text{Precision} \times \text{Recall}}{\text{Precision} + \text{Recall}}F1 Score=2×Precision+RecallPrecision×Recall

o **Example**: When both precision and recall are equally important, the F1 score offers a better measure than either alone.

```python
from sklearn.metrics import f1_score
f1 = f1_score(y_test, y_pred)
```

These metrics provide different perspectives on how the model performs, and understanding when to prioritize one over another is key to building successful machine learning models.

Supervised learning is an essential aspect of machine learning, focusing on using labeled data to make predictions. In this chapter, you learned about the fundamental concepts of supervised learning, key algorithms, how to split data for training and testing, and important performance metrics. By mastering these concepts, you'll be well-prepared to build effective supervised learning models.

In the next chapter, we will explore **Regression Models**, where we will delve into specific techniques for predicting continuous values using supervised learning.

.

CHAPTER 6

REGRESSION MODELS: PREDICTING CONTINUOUS VALUES

Linear Regression: Concept and Implementation

Linear regression is one of the simplest and most widely used algorithms in supervised learning for predicting continuous values. The goal of linear regression is to model the relationship between a dependent variable (target) and one or more independent variables (features) by fitting a linear equation to the observed data.

In its simplest form, **simple linear regression** involves one independent variable and one dependent variable. The linear relationship between the two is modeled as a straight line, described by the equation:

$y = \beta_0 + \beta_1 x + \epsilon$

Where:

- y is the dependent variable (target),
- x is the independent variable (feature),

61

- $\beta 0$\beta_0$\beta 0$ is the y-intercept,
- $\beta 1$\beta_1$\beta 1$ is the slope (coefficient) of the line, and
- ϵ\epsilon$\epsilon$ is the error term.

When there are multiple independent variables, the model becomes **multiple linear regression**:

$$y=\beta 0+\beta 1x1+\beta 2x2+...+\beta nxn+\epsilon y = \beta_0 + \beta_1 x_1 + \beta_2 x_2 + ... + \beta_n x_n + \epsilon y=\beta 0+\beta 1x1+\beta 2x2+...+\beta nxn+\epsilon$$

Where each feature $x1,x2,...,xn x_1, x_2, ..., x_n x1,x2,...,xn$ has a corresponding coefficient $\beta 1,\beta 2,...,\beta n$\beta_1, \beta_2, ..., \beta_n$\beta 1,\beta 2,...,\beta n$.

The goal of linear regression is to find the coefficients $\beta 0,\beta 1,...,\beta n$\beta_0, \beta_1, ..., \beta_n$\beta 0,\beta 1,...,\beta n$ that minimize the difference between the predicted values and the actual target values.

Implementation:

```python
from       sklearn.linear_model       import
LinearRegression
from       sklearn.model_selection       import
train_test_split
import pandas as pd
```

```python
# Load data (assuming you have a dataset with
columns 'feature' and 'target')
data = pd.read_csv('data.csv')

# Split the data into features (X) and target (y)
X = data[['feature1', 'feature2']]   # Multiple
features
y = data['target']

# Split into training and testing sets
X_train, X_test, y_train, y_test =
train_test_split(X, y, test_size=0.2,
random_state=42)

# Instantiate and train the model
model = LinearRegression()
model.fit(X_train, y_train)

# Make predictions
y_pred = model.predict(X_test)

# Output the coefficients
print("Intercept:", model.intercept_)
print("Coefficients:", model.coef_)
```

Polynomial Regression

Polynomial regression is an extension of linear regression that allows the model to fit a non-linear relationship between the dependent and independent variables. Instead of fitting a straight line, polynomial regression fits a polynomial equation to the data, making it capable of modeling more complex, curvilinear relationships.

The equation for a polynomial regression of degree ddd is:

y=β0+β1x+β2x2+β3x3+...+βdxd+ϵy = \beta_0 + \beta_1 x + \beta_2 x^2 + \beta_3 x^3 + ... + \beta_d x^d + \epsilony=β0+β1 x+β2x2+β3x3+...+βdxd+ϵ

Where xxx is raised to higher powers (squared, cubed, etc.), making the model more flexible.

Why Use Polynomial Regression?

- It is used when the relationship between the features and the target is non-linear.
- It provides a better fit when data shows a curvilinear trend.

Implementation:

```python
```

```
from          sklearn.preprocessing          import
PolynomialFeatures
from          sklearn.linear_model          import
LinearRegression
```

```python
# Load data (assuming you have 'feature' and
'target')
data = pd.read_csv('data.csv')
X = data[['feature']]   # Only one feature for
simplicity
y = data['target']

# Create polynomial features
poly = PolynomialFeatures(degree=2)   # Degree 2
for quadratic regression
X_poly = poly.fit_transform(X)

# Fit the model
model = LinearRegression()
model.fit(X_poly, y)

# Make predictions
y_pred = model.predict(X_poly)

# Plot the results
import matplotlib.pyplot as plt
plt.scatter(X, y, color='blue')
plt.plot(X, y_pred, color='red')
plt.title('Polynomial Regression (Degree 2)')
plt.xlabel('Feature')
plt.ylabel('Target')
plt.show()
```

In this example, we transformed the input feature into a quadratic form and trained a linear regression model on the transformed features. The resulting plot will show a curve, which represents the non-linear relationship between the feature and the target variable.

Evaluating Regression Models: MSE, RMSE, R-squared

Once we've trained a regression model, we need to evaluate its performance. There are several common metrics for evaluating regression models:

1. **Mean Squared Error (MSE)**:
   o MSE measures the average of the squares of the errors (the difference between predicted and actual values). It penalizes larger errors more than smaller ones due to squaring.
   o **Formula**:

   $$MSE = \frac{1}{n} \sum_{i=1}^{n} (y_i - \hat{y_i})^2$$

   Where y_i is the actual value, and $\hat{y_i}$ is the predicted value.

2. **Implementation:**
3. `python`

4.
5. `from         sklearn.metrics         import mean_squared_error`
6. `mse = mean_squared_error(y_test, y_pred)`
7. `print("Mean Squared Error:", mse)`
8. **Root Mean Squared Error (RMSE)**:
   - RMSE is simply the square root of the MSE. It's in the same unit as the target variable, making it easier to interpret.
   - **Formula**:

   $$RMSE = MSE RMSE = \sqrt{MSE} RMSE = MSE$$

9. **Implementation**:
10. `python`
11.
12. `import numpy as np`
13. `rmse = np.sqrt(mse)`
14. `print("Root Mean Squared Error:", rmse)`
15. **R-squared ($R2R^2R2$)**:
   - R-squared is a metric that tells us how well our model explains the variance in the target variable. It ranges from 0 to 1, where 1 indicates perfect prediction and 0 indicates no predictive power.
   - **Formula**:

   $$R2 = 1 - \frac{\sum i=1n(yi-yi^\wedge)2}{\sum i=1n(yi-y^-)2} R^2 = 1 - \frac{\sum_{i=1}^{n}}{} (y_i -$$

$\hat{y_i})^2}{\sum_{i=1}^{n}$ (y_i -
$\bar{y})^2}R2=1-\sum i=1n(yi-y^-)2\sum i=1n(yi-yi^$
)2

Where $y^-\bar{y}y^-$ is the mean of the actual values.

16. **Implementation:**
17. python
18.
19. from sklearn.metrics import r2_score
20. r2 = r2_score(y_test, y_pred)
21. print("R-squared:", r2)

Real-World Example: Predicting House Prices

One of the classic applications of regression is predicting house prices. For example, you might want to predict the price of a house based on various features like the number of rooms, square footage, location, etc. Let's walk through a simple example of predicting house prices using linear regression.

Step-by-step Example:

1. **Load the dataset**: The dataset might contain features such as square footage, number of bedrooms, and age of the house, along with the target variable, which is the house price.

2. **Preprocess the data**: Clean any missing values, normalize the features if necessary, and split the data into training and testing sets.

3. **Train a linear regression model**: Use the training data to build a model that learns the relationship between the features and the target.

4. **Evaluate the model**: Use MSE, RMSE, and R-squared to measure how well the model performs on the test set.

Code Example:

```python
python

# Load data (Assume a 'house_prices.csv' file
with features and target 'price')
data = pd.read_csv('house_prices.csv')

# Split the data into features and target
X = data[['square_feet', 'num_rooms', 'age']]  #
Features
y = data['price']  # Target variable

# Split into training and testing sets
X_train,    X_test,    y_train,    y_test    =
train_test_split(X,     y,      test_size=0.2,
random_state=42)

# Train the model
model = LinearRegression()
```

```
model.fit(X_train, y_train)

# Make predictions
y_pred = model.predict(X_test)

# Evaluate the model
mse = mean_squared_error(y_test, y_pred)
rmse = np.sqrt(mse)
r2 = r2_score(y_test, y_pred)

print(f"MSE: {mse}")
print(f"RMSE: {rmse}")
print(f"R-squared: {r2}")
```

In this example, we predict the price of a house based on features such as square footage, number of rooms, and age. The evaluation metrics (MSE, RMSE, and R-squared) help us assess the accuracy of the model and how well it generalizes to new data.

In this chapter, we've covered the fundamentals of regression models, including linear and polynomial regression, and discussed how to evaluate the performance of regression models using key metrics such as MSE, RMSE, and R-squared. Regression models, particularly linear regression, are foundational tools for predicting continuous values, and understanding their implementation and evaluation is critical for any machine learning practitioner.

In the next chapter, we will explore **Classification Models** and learn how to predict categorical outcomes using supervised learning techniques.

CHAPTER 7

CLASSIFICATION MODELS: CATEGORIZING DATA

What is Classification?

Classification is a type of supervised learning where the goal is to predict a categorical label for a given input. In other words, the model is tasked with assigning a class (or category) to a data point based on its features. Unlike regression, where the output is continuous, classification involves predicting discrete labels such as "yes/no," "spam/ham," or "cat/dog."

Classification is used in many real-world applications, such as:

- **Spam detection**: Classifying emails as spam or not spam.
- **Medical diagnosis**: Classifying patients as having a disease or not based on their symptoms and test results.
- **Image recognition**: Classifying images into categories such as animals, objects, or landscapes.

The key challenge in classification problems is that the data is divided into discrete classes, and the model must learn the decision boundaries that separate these classes based on the features provided.

Logistic Regression and its Use Cases

Logistic regression is one of the most commonly used algorithms for binary classification tasks. Despite the name, it is used for classification, not regression. It models the probability that a given input belongs to a particular class. The output is a value between 0 and 1, interpreted as the probability of belonging to the positive class.

The **logistic function** (also known as the sigmoid function) is used to map predicted values to probabilities:

$$P(y=1|X) = \frac{1}{1 + e^{-(\beta_0 + \beta_1 X_1 + \beta_2 X_2 + \dots + \beta_n X_n)}}$$

Where:

- $P(y=1|X)$ is the probability that the input belongs to class 1,
- $X_1, X_2, \dots, X_n$ are the input features,
- $\beta_0, \beta_1, \dots, \beta_n$ are the learned model coefficients.

Use Cases:

- **Spam Detection**: Classifying emails as "spam" or "not spam."
- **Loan Approval**: Predicting whether a loan application will be approved based on financial features.

Implementation:

python

```
from        sklearn.linear_model         import
LogisticRegression
from        sklearn.model_selection         import
train_test_split
from sklearn.metrics import accuracy_score

# Assume data contains 'feature1', 'feature2',
and 'target' (binary)
data = pd.read_csv('data.csv')
X = data[['feature1', 'feature2']]
y = data['target']

# Split data into training and testing sets
X_train,    X_test,    y_train,    y_test    =
train_test_split(X,       y,       test_size=0.2,
random_state=42)

# Initialize and train the logistic regression
model
model = LogisticRegression()
```

```
model.fit(X_train, y_train)

# Predict on test data
y_pred = model.predict(X_test)

# Evaluate the model
accuracy = accuracy_score(y_test, y_pred)
print(f'Accuracy: {accuracy}')
```

Decision Trees and Random Forests

Decision Trees: A decision tree is a supervised learning algorithm that recursively splits the dataset based on the feature that provides the best separation between the target classes. Each split corresponds to a decision rule based on one feature, and the process continues until the data can be perfectly classified or a stopping criterion is met.

A decision tree can be visualized as a flowchart, where:

- Each internal node represents a decision (splitting feature),
- Each branch represents an outcome of that decision,
- Each leaf node represents a class label.

Example Use Case: Classifying whether a customer will buy a product based on features like age, income, and previous purchase behavior.

75

Random Forests: Random forests are an ensemble method that builds multiple decision trees and combines their predictions. Each tree in the forest is trained on a random subset of the data, and the final prediction is made by averaging the predictions (for regression) or using majority voting (for classification).

Random forests overcome some of the limitations of decision trees, such as overfitting, by averaging over multiple trees, leading to better generalization.

Implementation of Decision Tree:

```python

from sklearn.tree import DecisionTreeClassifier

# Initialize and train the decision tree model
model = DecisionTreeClassifier(random_state=42)
model.fit(X_train, y_train)

# Predict on test data
y_pred = model.predict(X_test)

# Evaluate the model
accuracy = accuracy_score(y_test, y_pred)
print(f'Accuracy: {accuracy}')
```

Implementation of Random Forest:

```python
python

from            sklearn.ensemble            import
RandomForestClassifier

# Initialize and train the random forest model
model = RandomForestClassifier(random_state=42)
model.fit(X_train, y_train)

# Predict on test data
y_pred = model.predict(X_test)

# Evaluate the model
accuracy = accuracy_score(y_test, y_pred)
print(f'Accuracy: {accuracy}')
```

Evaluating Classification Models: Confusion Matrix, ROC Curve

To evaluate the performance of classification models, we use various metrics and plots that help us understand how well the model is performing, especially when dealing with imbalanced datasets.

1. **Confusion Matrix**: A confusion matrix is a table that compares the predicted labels with the actual labels. It shows the following:

    o **True Positives (TP)**: Correctly predicted positive class.

77

- o **True Negatives (TN)**: Correctly predicted negative class.

- o **False Positives (FP)**: Incorrectly predicted positive class (Type I error).

- o **False Negatives (FN)**: Incorrectly predicted negative class (Type II error).

The confusion matrix helps us calculate various metrics like accuracy, precision, recall, and F1 score.

Example:

```python
```

```python
from          sklearn.metrics          import
confusion_matrix
cm = confusion_matrix(y_test, y_pred)
print(cm)
```

You can also visualize the confusion matrix using a heatmap:

```python
```

```python
import seaborn as sns
sns.heatmap(cm,      annot=True,      fmt='d',
cmap='Blues',      xticklabels=['Negative',
'Positive'],      yticklabels=['Negative',
'Positive'])
```

Understanding Machine Learning

```
plt.title('Confusion Matrix')
plt.show()
```

2. **ROC Curve (Receiver Operating Characteristic Curve)**: The ROC curve is a graphical representation of the performance of a classification model at various thresholds. The curve plots the **True Positive Rate (TPR)** against the **False Positive Rate (FPR)**.

   o **True Positive Rate (TPR)**: Also known as recall or sensitivity, it represents the proportion of actual positives correctly identified by the model.

   o **False Positive Rate (FPR)**: The proportion of actual negatives incorrectly identified as positive by the model.

The ROC curve helps evaluate the trade-off between sensitivity and specificity and is particularly useful for imbalanced datasets.

Example:

```
python
```

```
from sklearn.metrics import roc_curve, auc
fpr, tpr, thresholds = roc_curve(y_test,
model.predict_proba(X_test)[:, 1])
roc_auc = auc(fpr, tpr)
```

79

```
# Plot the ROC curve
plt.plot(fpr,   tpr,   color='darkorange',
lw=2,  label='ROC  curve  (area´=  %0.2f)'  %
roc_auc)
plt.plot([0,   1],   [0,   1],   color='navy',
lw=2, linestyle='--')
plt.xlabel('False Positive Rate')
plt.ylabel('True Positive Rate')
plt.title('Receiver              Operating
Characteristic (ROC) Curve')
plt.legend(loc='lower right')
plt.show()
```

Real-World Example: Spam Email Detection

Spam email detection is a classic example of a binary classification problem. The goal is to classify an email as either "spam" or "not spam" based on its features, such as the sender, subject, content, and any other relevant attributes.

Steps:

1. **Dataset**: You can use a dataset like the **SpamAssassin** dataset or **Enron spam** dataset, which contains labeled examples of emails classified as spam or not spam.

2. **Preprocessing**: Clean the data, remove stopwords, and convert text features into numerical values using methods like **TF-IDF** or **Bag of Words**.

80

3. **Model Training**: Train a classification model, such as logistic regression or decision trees, on the dataset.

4. **Model Evaluation**: Use metrics like accuracy, confusion matrix, and ROC curve to assess the performance of the model.

Implementation:

python

```
from    sklearn.feature_extraction.text    import
TfidfVectorizer
from        sklearn.model_selection        import
train_test_split
from            sklearn.linear_model        import
LogisticRegression

# Load dataset
data = pd.read_csv('spam_emails.csv')
X = data['email_content']
y = data['label']

# Convert email content to numerical features
using TF-IDF
vectorizer                                    =
TfidfVectorizer(stop_words='english')
X_tfidf = vectorizer.fit_transform(X)

# Split the data into training and testing sets
```

81

```
X_train,      X_test,      y_train,      y_test      =
train_test_split(X_tfidf,   y,   test_size=0.2,
random_state=42)

# Train a logistic regression model
model = LogisticRegression()
model.fit(X_train, y_train)

# Predict on test data
y_pred = model.predict(X_test)

# Evaluate the model
accuracy = accuracy_score(y_test, y_pred)
print(f'Accuracy: {accuracy}')
```

In this chapter, we covered the fundamental concepts of classification, including logistic regression, decision trees, and random forests. We also explored essential evaluation metrics like confusion matrices, ROC curves, and accuracy. With a real-world example of spam email detection, you've learned how to apply classification models to a practical problem.

In the next chapter, we'll explore **Clustering and Unsupervised Learning**, where we will focus on techniques for discovering patterns in data without labeled outcomes.

CHAPTER 8

MODEL EVALUATION AND HYPERPARAMETER TUNING

Cross-Validation: K-Fold, Leave-One-Out

Cross-validation is an essential technique for assessing the performance of machine learning models, especially when dealing with limited data. It helps evaluate how well a model generalizes to an independent dataset, preventing overfitting and ensuring robustness.

1. **K-Fold Cross-Validation**:
    o   In K-Fold cross-validation, the dataset is divided into "K" equal-sized subsets or folds. The model is trained on $K-1$ $K-1$ $K-1$ folds and tested on the remaining fold. This process is repeated KKK times, each time using a different fold for testing and the remaining folds for training.
    o   The final performance metric is the average of the KKK results. K-Fold cross-validation ensures that every data point is used for both training and testing, providing a more reliable estimate of model performance.

83

Example:

```python
from    sklearn.model_selection    import
cross_val_score
from        sklearn.ensemble       import
RandomForestClassifier

# Initialize model
model = RandomForestClassifier()

# Apply 5-Fold cross-validation
scores = cross_val_score(model, X, y, cv=5)
# cv=5 denotes 5 folds
print("Cross-Validation Scores:", scores)
print("Mean    Cross-Validation    Score:",
scores.mean())
```

In this example, the model is evaluated using 5-fold cross-validation, and the average score is computed to estimate its performance.

2. **Leave-One-Out Cross-Validation (LOO-CV)**:
   - o Leave-One-Out Cross-Validation (LOO-CV) is a special case of K-Fold cross-validation where KKK equals the number of data points in the dataset. For each fold, only one data point is used

for testing, and the model is trained on all other data points.

- o LOO-CV is computationally expensive, especially for large datasets, but it provides an almost unbiased estimate of model performance.

Example:

```python

from sklearn.model_selection import LeaveOneOut

# Initialize the Leave-One-Out cross-validator
loo = LeaveOneOut()

# Apply LOO-CV to the model
scores = cross_val_score(model, X, y, cv=loo)
print("Leave-One-Out Scores:", scores)
print("Mean Leave-One-Out Score:", scores.mean())
```

Grid Search and Randomized Search

Both **Grid Search** and **Randomized Search** are techniques used to find the best combination of hyperparameters for a machine learning model. These methods help in improving the model's performance by systematically searching for optimal parameter values.

1. **Grid Search**:
   - Grid search exhaustively tests all possible combinations of specified hyperparameters. It is computationally expensive but guarantees that the best combination is found within the specified grid.
   - **Example**: You might want to tune hyperparameters like the number of trees in a Random Forest, or the regularization parameter in a Logistic Regression.

Implementation of Grid Search:

python

```python
from sklearn.model_selection import GridSearchCV
from sklearn.ensemble import RandomForestClassifier

# Define the model
model = RandomForestClassifier()

# Define the parameter grid
param_grid = {
```

```
    'n_estimators': [50, 100, 150],    #
Number of trees in the forest
    'max_depth': [5, 10, 15],          # Max
depth of the tree
    'min_samples_split': [2, 5, 10]  # Min
number of samples required to split a node
}

# Initialize GridSearchCV
grid_search                              =
GridSearchCV(estimator=model,
param_grid=param_grid, cv=5, n_jobs=-1)

# Fit grid search to the data
grid_search.fit(X_train, y_train)

# Print the best parameters and score
print("Best                Parameters:",
grid_search.best_params_)
print("Best                     Score:",
grid_search.best_score_)
```

In this example, the grid search tests all combinations of the hyperparameters defined in the `param_grid` dictionary, and the best combination is selected based on cross-validation performance.

2. **Randomized Search**:

87

- o Randomized search is a more efficient alternative to grid search. Instead of testing all combinations of hyperparameters, it samples a fixed number of hyperparameter combinations from the specified ranges. It's useful when you have a large hyperparameter space and computational resources are limited.
- o Randomized search may not guarantee the optimal combination but can often find a good enough solution with less computation.

Implementation of Randomized Search:

python

```
from       sklearn.model_selection       import
RandomizedSearchCV
from         sklearn.ensemble          import
RandomForestClassifier
import numpy as np

# Define the model
model = RandomForestClassifier()

# Define the parameter distribution
param_dist = {
    'n_estimators':   np.arange(50,   201,
50),   # Range for the number of trees
```

88

```
    'max_depth':   [5,   10,   15,   None],
# Max depth of the trees
    'min_samples_split':   [2,   5,   10]
# Min number of samples to split
}

# Initialize RandomizedSearchCV
randomized_search                              =
RandomizedSearchCV(estimator=model,
param_distributions=param_dist,
n_iter=100, cv=5, n_jobs=-1)

# Fit randomized search to the data
randomized_search.fit(X_train, y_train)

# Print the best parameters and score
print("Best                Parameters:",
randomized_search.best_params_)
print("Best                Score:",
randomized_search.best_score_)
```

This example randomly samples 100 different combinations of hyperparameters from the parameter distribution and selects the best one based on cross-validation performance.

Bias-Variance Tradeoff

The **bias-variance tradeoff** is one of the most important concepts in machine learning. It describes the relationship between two types of errors that a model can make:

- **Bias**: The error introduced by approximating a real-world problem, which may be complex, by a simplified model. High bias occurs when the model is too simple and fails to capture the underlying patterns (underfitting).
- **Variance**: The error introduced by the model's sensitivity to small fluctuations in the training data. High variance occurs when the model is too complex and overfits the training data.
- **Overfitting**: When the model has low bias but high variance, it fits the training data very well but performs poorly on new, unseen data.
- **Underfitting**: When the model has high bias and low variance, it fails to capture the patterns in the data, leading to poor performance on both training and testing datasets.

The goal of a good machine learning model is to find the right balance between bias and variance, minimizing the total error.

Visualizing the Tradeoff:

python

```python
import matplotlib.pyplot as plt
import numpy as np

# Example: Bias-Variance Tradeoff
x = np.linspace(0, 10, 100)
y_true = np.sin(x)   # True underlying function

# Hypothetical models with increasing complexity
model_1 = 0.1 * x + 1  # High bias, low variance
(underfitting)
model_2 = 0.5 * x + 2  # Moderate bias, moderate
variance
model_3 = np.sin(x)   # Low bias, low variance
(perfect fit)
model_4 = x**3 - 10*x  # High variance, low bias
(overfitting)

# Plotting
plt.plot(x,   y_true,   label='True   Function',
color='black')
plt.plot(x, model_1, label='Model 1 (High Bias)',
color='blue')
plt.plot(x,  model_2,  label='Model  2  (Moderate
Bias)', color='green')
plt.plot(x, model_3, label='Model 3 (Low Bias)',
color='red')
plt.plot(x,   model_4,   label='Model   4   (High
Variance)', color='purple')
plt.legend()
```

```
plt.title("Bias-Variance Tradeoff")
plt.xlabel("x")
plt.ylabel("y")
plt.show()
```

In this plot, **Model 1** and **Model 4** represent extremes of high bias and high variance, respectively. **Model 3** shows the ideal case where the bias and variance are both minimized.

Hyperparameter Tuning with Scikit-learn

Hyperparameter tuning is the process of selecting the best combination of hyperparameters for a given model. In Scikit-learn, hyperparameter tuning can be efficiently done using **GridSearchCV** and **RandomizedSearchCV**, both of which we've discussed.

You can also use the `best_params_` attribute to access the best hyperparameters found during the search:

```python
python

# After performing grid or randomized search
best_model = grid_search.best_estimator_

# Use the best model for predictions
y_pred = best_model.predict(X_test)
```

This step ensures that the model is fine-tuned to achieve the best performance based on the training data and the validation process.

In this chapter, we covered key techniques for model evaluation and improvement:

- **Cross-validation**: Methods like K-fold and leave-one-out help ensure that the model generalizes well.
- **Hyperparameter tuning**: Grid search and randomized search enable the selection of the best model parameters.
- **Bias-variance tradeoff**: Understanding and managing bias and variance is key to building effective models.
- **Tuning in Scikit-learn**: Hyperparameter optimization using built-in tools in Scikit-learn.

With these tools and techniques, you are now better equipped to evaluate your models thoroughly and optimize them for better performance. In the next chapter, we'll explore **Clustering and Unsupervised Learning**, where we focus on uncovering hidden patterns in data without labeled outcomes.

CHAPTER 9

CLUSTERING AND UNSUPERVISED LEARNING

What is Unsupervised Learning?

Unsupervised learning is a type of machine learning where the model is trained on data without labeled outputs. Unlike supervised learning, which relies on data that includes both input features and the corresponding labels (targets), unsupervised learning seeks to identify patterns, structures, or relationships in data that has no predefined labels.

The primary goal of unsupervised learning is to explore the inherent structure of the data, find similarities between data points, and group them accordingly. Some common unsupervised learning techniques include clustering and dimensionality reduction.

Key Applications of Unsupervised Learning:

- **Clustering**: Grouping similar data points together.
- **Anomaly Detection**: Identifying rare data points that do not fit the general pattern.
- **Dimensionality Reduction**: Reducing the number of features in the data while retaining important information.

94

In this chapter, we will focus on **clustering**—a technique used to group similar data points together—and explore some of the most popular clustering algorithms.

K-Means Clustering

K-Means is one of the most widely used clustering algorithms. It partitions the data into KKK distinct clusters based on feature similarity. The algorithm works by assigning data points to the nearest centroid (the mean of all data points in a cluster) and iteratively updating the centroids until convergence.

Steps of K-Means Clustering:

1. **Initialize centroids**: Select KKK initial centroids randomly.
2. **Assign points to the nearest centroid**: Each data point is assigned to the closest centroid.
3. **Update centroids**: After the points are assigned, the centroids are recalculated as the mean of all data points in the cluster.
4. **Repeat steps 2 and 3**: Continue until the centroids do not change significantly (i.e., convergence).

Choosing the Right Value for KKK: The number of clusters, KKK, is a hyperparameter that must be chosen before training. One common method for selecting KKK is the **Elbow Method**, which looks at the plot of the sum of squared distances between data points and their respective centroids (inertia). The "elbow" of the curve indicates the optimal KKK value.

Implementation of K-Means Clustering:

python

```python
from sklearn.cluster import KMeans
import matplotlib.pyplot as plt

# Assume data is a DataFrame with two features
X = data[['feature1', 'feature2']]

# Apply K-Means clustering
kmeans = KMeans(n_clusters=3, random_state=42)  # Assume K=3
kmeans.fit(X)

# Predict the cluster labels
y_pred = kmeans.predict(X)

# Plot the clusters
plt.scatter(X['feature1'],        X['feature2'],
c=y_pred, cmap='viridis')
plt.scatter(kmeans.cluster_centers_[:,        0],
kmeans.cluster_centers_[:, 1], s=300, c='red',
marker='x')
plt.title("K-Means Clustering")
plt.xlabel("Feature 1")
```

```
plt.ylabel("Feature 2")
plt.show()
```

In this example, the K-Means algorithm groups the data points into 3 clusters, with the red crosses indicating the centroids.

Hierarchical Clustering

Hierarchical clustering is another popular clustering technique that builds a tree-like structure called a **dendrogram**, which illustrates how the data points are clustered together at various levels of similarity. The two main approaches for hierarchical clustering are:

1. **Agglomerative** (bottom-up approach): Starts with each data point as its own cluster and merges the closest pairs of clusters until only one cluster remains.
2. **Divisive** (top-down approach): Starts with all data points in a single cluster and recursively splits the data into smaller clusters.

Dendrogram: The dendrogram visualizes the hierarchy of clusters. It shows at which level of the tree clusters are merged or divided, with the vertical axis representing the distance or dissimilarity between clusters.

Implementation of Hierarchical Clustering (Agglomerative):

97

python

```
from           sklearn.cluster           import
AgglomerativeClustering
import scipy.cluster.hierarchy as sch

# Apply Agglomerative Clustering
hierarchical_model                             =
AgglomerativeClustering(n_clusters=3,
linkage='ward')    #  'ward'  minimizes  variance
within clusters
y_pred = hierarchical_model.fit_predict(X)

# Plot the dendrogram
dendrogram    =    sch.dendrogram(sch.linkage(X,
method='ward'))
plt.title("Dendrogram      for      Hierarchical
Clustering")
plt.xlabel("Data Points")
plt.ylabel("Distance")
plt.show()
```

In this example, hierarchical clustering is applied to the data, and the dendrogram visualizes how the data points are merged into clusters.

DBSCAN and Density-Based Clustering

DBSCAN (Density-Based Spatial Clustering of Applications with Noise) is a clustering algorithm that groups data points based on their density. Unlike K-Means, DBSCAN does not require the user to specify the number of clusters in advance. Instead, it relies on two key parameters:

- **Epsilon (ϵ\epsilonϵ)**: The maximum distance between two points for them to be considered part of the same neighborhood.
- **MinPts**: The minimum number of points required to form a dense region (i.e., a cluster).

Key Characteristics:

- **Noise**: DBSCAN can identify and handle noise (outliers) in the data, which K-Means cannot do effectively.
- **Non-spherical clusters**: DBSCAN can detect clusters of arbitrary shapes, whereas K-Means assumes spherical clusters.

Implementation of DBSCAN:

```python
python

from sklearn.cluster import DBSCAN
```

```
# Apply DBSCAN clustering
dbscan = DBSCAN(eps=0.5, min_samples=5)
y_pred = dbscan.fit_predict(X)

# Plot the clusters
plt.scatter(X['feature1'],        X['feature2'],
c=y_pred, cmap='viridis')
plt.title("DBSCAN Clustering")
plt.xlabel("Feature 1")
plt.ylabel("Feature 2")
plt.show()
```

In this example, DBSCAN identifies the clusters, with noise points marked as -1. The plot visualizes the detected clusters and noise.

Real-World Example: Customer Segmentation

Customer segmentation is a common application of clustering in marketing. The goal is to group customers based on similar behavior, demographics, or preferences, allowing businesses to tailor their marketing strategies accordingly.

Steps for Customer Segmentation:

1. **Dataset**: Assume we have a dataset containing customer attributes such as age, income, spending score, etc.
2. **Preprocessing**: Clean the data, normalize the features, and handle missing values.

100

3. **Clustering**: Apply a clustering algorithm (e.g., K-Means or DBSCAN) to segment customers into distinct groups.

4. **Interpretation**: Analyze the resulting clusters to understand customer characteristics and behavior.

Implementation Example for Customer Segmentation with K-Means:

python

```
# Load customer data (assuming
'customer_data.csv' contains features like
'age', 'income', 'spending_score')
customer_data = pd.read_csv('customer_data.csv')

# Select relevant features
X = customer_data[['age', 'income',
'spending_score']]

# Normalize the data (important for K-Means)
from sklearn.preprocessing import StandardScaler
scaler = StandardScaler()
X_scaled = scaler.fit_transform(X)

# Apply K-Means clustering
kmeans = KMeans(n_clusters=4, random_state=42)  #
Assume we want 4 segments
kmeans.fit(X_scaled)
```

```
# Assign cluster labels
customer_data['Cluster'] = kmeans.labels_

# Visualize the clusters
plt.scatter(customer_data['age'],
customer_data['income'],
c=customer_data['Cluster'], cmap='viridis')
plt.title("Customer    Segmentation    (Age    vs
Income)")
plt.xlabel("Age")
plt.ylabel("Income")
plt.show()
```

In this example, K-Means is used to segment customers based on their age, income, and spending score. The resulting plot shows how customers are grouped into four distinct clusters, each representing a different customer segment.

In this chapter, we covered the essentials of unsupervised learning, focusing on clustering algorithms. We explored **K-Means**, **Hierarchical Clustering**, and **DBSCAN**, and we saw how clustering can be applied to a real-world problem such as **customer segmentation**. Understanding these clustering techniques will help you uncover hidden patterns in your data, making it possible to make more informed decisions based on the structure of your dataset.

In the next chapter, we will explore **Dimensionality Reduction**, a technique that can help simplify complex data and improve the performance of machine learning models by reducing the number of features.

CHAPTER 10

DIMENSIONALITY REDUCTION AND FEATURE SELECTION

Why is Dimensionality Reduction Important?

Dimensionality reduction is a crucial step in the data preprocessing pipeline, particularly when working with high-dimensional datasets. As the number of features (dimensions) increases, the complexity of the data grows, leading to several challenges:

- **Overfitting**: High-dimensional data can lead to overfitting, where the model captures noise rather than the underlying patterns.
- **Computational Efficiency**: More features require more memory and processing power, which can slow down model training and prediction.
- **Data Visualization**: High-dimensional data is difficult to visualize. Reducing the number of dimensions helps in better understanding and exploring the data.

By reducing the number of dimensions (features) while retaining the most important information, dimensionality reduction helps in:

- **Reducing Overfitting**: Fewer features mean the model is less likely to memorize the training data.
- **Improving Performance**: Removing irrelevant or redundant features can improve model accuracy and reduce training time.
- **Simplifying Models**: A simpler model is often easier to interpret and analyze.

Dimensionality reduction is particularly useful when dealing with datasets that have hundreds or thousands of features, which is common in fields like genomics, image processing, and text mining.

Principal Component Analysis (PCA)

Principal Component Analysis (PCA) is one of the most popular techniques for dimensionality reduction. PCA works by transforming the original features into a new set of features called **principal components**. These components are linear combinations of the original features and are ordered by the amount of variance they explain in the data. The first principal component explains the most variance, the second explains the second-most variance, and so on.

Why Use PCA?

- **Unsupervised Learning**: PCA is an unsupervised method, meaning it doesn't require labeled data.

105

- **Reducing Complexity**: PCA helps simplify complex datasets by finding new features that summarize the most important information.
- **Preserving Variance**: PCA aims to reduce dimensionality while retaining as much variance (information) as possible from the original data.

How PCA Works:

1. **Standardize the Data**: Since PCA is affected by the scale of the features, it is essential to standardize the data to have zero mean and unit variance.
2. **Compute the Covariance Matrix**: This matrix describes the variance and correlation between the features.
3. **Calculate Eigenvalues and Eigenvectors**: The eigenvectors represent the new axes (principal components), and the eigenvalues tell us the amount of variance captured by each component.
4. **Sort and Select Principal Components**: Select the top kkk components that explain the most variance, where kkk is the desired number of dimensions.

Implementation of PCA:

python

```
from sklearn.decomposition import PCA
from sklearn.preprocessing import StandardScaler
```

```python
import matplotlib.pyplot as plt

# Load data
data = pd.read_csv('data.csv')
X = data[['feature1', 'feature2', 'feature3',
'feature4']]  # Select relevant features

# Standardize the data
scaler = StandardScaler()
X_scaled = scaler.fit_transform(X)

# Apply PCA
pca = PCA(n_components=2)      # Reduce to 2
components
X_pca = pca.fit_transform(X_scaled)

# Visualize the results
plt.scatter(X_pca[:, 0], X_pca[:, 1], c='blue',
edgecolor='k', alpha=0.7)
plt.title("PCA:   2D   Projection   of   High-
Dimensional Data")
plt.xlabel("Principal Component 1")
plt.ylabel("Principal Component 2")
plt.show()
```

In this example, PCA reduces the dimensionality of the data from four features to two principal components. The plot shows the data points in the new 2D space, where the most important variance in the data is captured by the two principal components.

Feature Selection Techniques: Recursive Feature Elimination, L1 Regularization

Feature selection is the process of selecting the most relevant features from the dataset, while discarding the less important ones. This helps in reducing model complexity, improving performance, and mitigating overfitting. Below are some common feature selection techniques:

1. **Recursive Feature Elimination (RFE)**: RFE is a wrapper method that recursively removes the least important features based on the model's performance. It starts with all features, trains a model, ranks the features based on importance (e.g., using coefficients for linear models or feature importance for tree-based models), and removes the least important ones. This process is repeated until the desired number of features is reached.

   Implementation of RFE:

   ```python
   from sklearn.feature_selection import RFE
   from sklearn.linear_model import LogisticRegression

   # Initialize the model
   model = LogisticRegression()
   ```

```
# Initialize the RFE method (selecting 3
features)
rfe = RFE(model, n_features_to_select=3)
X_rfe    =    rfe.fit_transform(X_train,
y_train)

# Print the selected features
print("Selected              Features:",
X.columns[rfe.support_])
```

In this example, RFE selects the top 3 features from the dataset based on the logistic regression model's performance.

2. **L1 Regularization (Lasso)**: L1 regularization, also known as Lasso (Least Absolute Shrinkage and Selection Operator), is a technique used for both feature selection and regularization. It penalizes the absolute magnitude of the coefficients, forcing some of them to zero. This naturally eliminates irrelevant features, making it a great tool for sparse feature selection.

Implementation of L1 Regularization (Lasso):

```
python

from sklearn.linear_model import Lasso
```

109

```
# Initialize the Lasso model with L1
regularization
lasso = Lasso(alpha=0.01)       # The
regularization strength
lasso.fit(X_train, y_train)

# Get the coefficients and the features
selected
selected_features = X.columns[lasso.coef_
!= 0]
print("Selected Features by Lasso:",
selected_features)
```

In this example, Lasso performs feature selection by penalizing the coefficients and selecting the most relevant features based on the magnitude of their coefficients.

Reducing Overfitting and Improving Model Performance

Dimensionality reduction and feature selection techniques help in reducing the complexity of the model, which in turn helps to **reduce overfitting**. When a model is overfitting, it has learned not only the underlying patterns but also the noise in the training data, which leads to poor generalization to unseen data.

1. **How Dimensionality Reduction Helps**: By removing redundant or irrelevant features, dimensionality reduction ensures that the model focuses on the most important

aspects of the data, preventing overfitting and improving its ability to generalize.

2. **How Feature Selection Helps**: Feature selection helps by ensuring that the model uses only the most relevant features, which can reduce the model's complexity and improve its performance on new data. Both **RFE** and **Lasso** techniques help eliminate noisy or irrelevant features, leading to better generalization.

Example: Overfitting vs. Regularization

```python
python

from sklearn.model_selection import cross_val_score
from sklearn.linear_model import Lasso

# Train a model without regularization (no feature selection)
model_no_reg = LogisticRegression()
scores_no_reg = cross_val_score(model_no_reg, X_train, y_train, cv=5)

# Train a model with Lasso regularization
model_lasso = Lasso(alpha=0.01)
scores_lasso = cross_val_score(model_lasso, X_train, y_train, cv=5)

# Compare the results
```

111

```
print(f"Accuracy      without      regularization:
{scores_no_reg.mean()}")
print(f"Accuracy   with   Lasso   regularization:
{scores_lasso.mean()}")
```

In this example, the accuracy of the model with Lasso regularization will likely be higher because Lasso reduces overfitting by selecting only the most relevant features.

In this chapter, we've explored the importance of dimensionality reduction and feature selection in machine learning. Techniques like **PCA, RFE**, and **Lasso** allow us to reduce the complexity of our models, improving performance and mitigating overfitting. By carefully selecting features and reducing dimensions, we make our models more efficient and capable of generalizing better to new data.

In the next chapter, we will dive into **Ensemble Methods**, which combine the predictions of multiple models to improve accuracy and robustness.

CHAPTER 11

NEURAL NETWORKS AND DEEP LEARNING

Introduction to Neural Networks

Neural networks are a fundamental component of deep learning and a powerful tool for solving a wide range of complex tasks, including image recognition, natural language processing, and game playing. A neural network is a computational model inspired by the way biological neurons in the human brain work. These models consist of layers of nodes, called **neurons**, that process information by passing it through layers and adjusting weights based on learned data patterns.

Neural networks have gained significant popularity due to their ability to learn from large amounts of data and their success in solving problems that traditional machine learning models struggle with. In particular, deep learning (a subset of neural networks with many layers) has revolutionized fields such as computer vision, speech recognition, and self-driving cars.

At the heart of a neural network is its ability to **learn representations** of data by adjusting the weights and biases of the connections between neurons based on feedback from the training data.

Structure of a Neural Network: Neurons, Layers, Weights

A typical neural network consists of the following components:

1. **Neurons**: Neurons are the building blocks of neural networks. They receive input data, apply a mathematical operation, and produce an output that is passed on to the next layer. Each neuron takes inputs from the previous layer, processes them, and sends the result to the next layer in the network.

2. **Layers**: A neural network consists of several layers:
    o **Input Layer**: The first layer of the network that receives the raw data. Each neuron in the input layer represents a feature in the dataset.
    o **Hidden Layers**: Layers between the input and output layers, where the actual computation happens. These layers learn the complex patterns and features of the data.
    o **Output Layer**: The final layer that produces the output (prediction). For classification tasks, this layer may consist of one or more neurons that represent the classes.

The depth of a network refers to the number of hidden layers. Deep neural networks, often referred to as **deep learning models**, have many hidden layers, allowing them to learn hierarchical representations of the data.

3. **Weights**: Weights are the parameters that control the strength of the connection between two neurons. Each connection between neurons has a weight that is adjusted during training to minimize the error between the predicted and actual output. The optimization process involves adjusting the weights using algorithms like **gradient descent**.

   Mathematically, each neuron's output is calculated by summing the weighted inputs and applying an activation function.

4. **Bias**: Bias is an additional parameter added to the weighted sum to allow the model to better fit the data. It enables the model to shift the activation function, making it more flexible.

Neural Network Diagram:

```
scss


Input Layer      Hidden Layer       Output Layer
   (X1) ──┐         (H1) ──┬──→  (O1)   (class 1)
```

(X2) ⌐┘ |
                            └──→ (O2)   (class 2)

- Each connection (X1 to H1, etc.) has a weight associated with it.

Activation Functions: ReLU, Sigmoid, Tanh

Activation functions are mathematical functions that determine whether a neuron should be activated or not. They introduce non-linearity into the network, allowing it to learn complex patterns.

1. **ReLU (Rectified Linear Unit)**: ReLU is the most commonly used activation function for hidden layers. It replaces any negative value with zero, while positive values remain unchanged:

   ReLU(x)=max⁣(0,x)\text{ReLU}(x)   =   \max(0, x)ReLU(x)=max(0,x)

   Why ReLU?: It is computationally efficient and helps mitigate the vanishing gradient problem during training. However, it can suffer from the "dying ReLU" problem, where neurons get stuck in the inactive state (output = 0).

   Example:

   ```python
   python
   ```

116

```
import numpy as np
def relu(x):
    return np.maximum(0, x)
```

2. **Sigmoid**: The sigmoid function maps input values to a range between 0 and 1, making it ideal for binary classification problems where the output is a probability.

$$\sigma(x) = \frac{1}{1 + e^{-x}}$$

Why Sigmoid?: It's useful for output layers of binary classification tasks, where the model predicts the probability of belonging to a certain class.

Example:

python

```
def sigmoid(x):
    return 1 / (1 + np.exp(-x))
```

3. **Tanh (Hyperbolic Tangent)**: The tanh function maps input values to a range between -1 and 1. It's similar to sigmoid but has a wider output range, making it useful for hidden layers.

$$\tanh(x) = \frac{e^{x} - e^{-x}}{e^{x} + e^{-x}}$$

117

Why Tanh?: It works well when the output of the neuron needs to be centered around 0, which can speed up training and lead to better convergence.

Example:

python

```
def tanh(x):
    return np.tanh(x)
```

Real-World Example: Image Classification

Image classification is a classic application of neural networks, where the goal is to classify images into one of several categories. Convolutional Neural Networks (CNNs) are typically used for image classification tasks, but here we will illustrate the basic idea of image classification using a simple feed-forward neural network.

Let's say we have a dataset of handwritten digits (e.g., MNIST), and the task is to classify each image as one of the digits from 0 to 9.

Steps:

1. **Data Preprocessing**: The image data must be normalized and reshaped to fit into the neural network model.

2. **Build a Neural Network**: We'll use a simple feed-forward neural network with one hidden layer.

3. **Train the Model**: The model will be trained using backpropagation to adjust the weights and minimize the loss function.

4. **Evaluate the Model**: The model's performance is evaluated using metrics such as accuracy.

Implementation Example (with TensorFlow/Keras):

```python
python

import tensorflow as tf
from tensorflow.keras import layers, models
from tensorflow.keras.datasets import mnist

# Load and preprocess the MNIST dataset
(x_train,    y_train),    (x_test,    y_test)    =
mnist.load_data()
x_train, x_test = x_train / 255.0, x_test / 255.0
# Normalize images

# Build a simple feed-forward neural network
model = models.Sequential([
    layers.Flatten(input_shape=(28,   28)),    #
Flatten the 28x28 images into 1D
    layers.Dense(128,   activation='relu'),    #
Hidden layer with ReLU activation
```

119

```
    layers.Dense(10,  activation='softmax')    #
Output layer for 10 classes (digits 0-9)
])

# Compile the model
model.compile(optimizer='adam',
loss='sparse_categorical_crossentropy',
metrics=['accuracy'])

# Train the model
model.fit(x_train, y_train, epochs=5)

# Evaluate the model on the test data
test_loss,  test_acc  =  model.evaluate(x_test,
y_test, verbose=2)
print(f"Test accuracy: {test_acc}")
```

In this example, we are using a simple feed-forward neural
network to classify images of handwritten digits. The model is
trained using the **Adam optimizer** and **sparse categorical cross-
entropy loss**, which is suitable for multi-class classification
problems.

Key Takeaways:

- **Neural Networks** are a powerful tool for solving
  complex tasks like image classification, natural language
  processing, and speech recognition.

120

- The structure of a neural network consists of **neurons, layers, weights**, and **biases**. The network learns by adjusting the weights during training.

- **Activation functions** like ReLU, sigmoid, and tanh introduce non-linearity, enabling the model to learn complex patterns.

- **Image classification** is a real-world example where neural networks, especially CNNs, excel in recognizing and categorizing images.

In the next chapter, we will explore **Convolutional Neural Networks (CNNs)** in detail, focusing on how they are specifically designed for image and spatial data processing.

CHAPTER 12

INTRODUCTION TO TENSORFLOW AND KERAS

Installing TensorFlow and Keras

TensorFlow is an open-source deep learning framework developed by Google. Keras, originally an independent high-level neural networks API, is now part of TensorFlow, providing an easy-to-use interface for building and training deep learning models.

To get started with TensorFlow and Keras, you need to install TensorFlow, which automatically includes Keras. You can install TensorFlow using **pip**:

1. **Installing TensorFlow**: To install TensorFlow and Keras, run the following command in your terminal or command prompt:

   ```
   bash
   ```

   ```
   pip install tensorflow
   ```

   This will install the latest version of TensorFlow, along with the Keras API.

2. **Verify the Installation**: After installation, verify that TensorFlow is correctly installed by running the following Python code:

```python
python

import tensorflow as tf
print("TensorFlow                    version:",
tf.__version__)
```

If TensorFlow is installed correctly, this command will print the version of TensorFlow you installed.

Overview of TensorFlow and Keras Frameworks

1. **TensorFlow**:
   - TensorFlow is a comprehensive machine learning framework that supports deep learning, but it can also handle other types of machine learning, such as reinforcement learning and classical machine learning. TensorFlow provides tools for model building, training, and deployment at scale.
   - It is optimized for high-performance computing, making it suitable for training large-scale neural networks on powerful hardware such as GPUs or TPUs (Tensor Processing Units).

123

TensorFlow is often used in production environments where model deployment, scalability, and performance are critical.

2. **Keras**:
   - o Keras is a high-level neural network API that makes it easy to build and train deep learning models. It was designed to simplify the process of building neural networks by providing user-friendly interfaces for defining and training models.
   - o Keras is now fully integrated into TensorFlow as the high-level API, so it can be used to define and train models in a straightforward and easy-to-understand way.
   - o Keras abstracts many of the underlying complexities of TensorFlow, allowing for faster development of deep learning models.

Key Keras components:

   - o **Models**: Define the architecture of your neural network.
   - o **Layers**: Create the individual components (e.g., fully connected layers, convolutional layers).

- o **Optimizers**: Algorithms that adjust the weights of the network to minimize the loss function during training.
- o **Loss Functions**: Functions that measure the error in predictions.
- o **Metrics**: Functions to evaluate the performance of the model.

Building a Simple Neural Network with Keras

Let's build a simple neural network using Keras to classify handwritten digits from the MNIST dataset, which contains 28x28 grayscale images of digits 0-9.

1. **Load the MNIST Dataset**: Keras includes a number of built-in datasets, including MNIST. You can load it with the following code:

```python
from tensorflow.keras.datasets import mnist

# Load the dataset (training and testing sets)
(x_train, y_train), (x_test, y_test) = mnist.load_data()
```

```
# Normalize the data to the range [0, 1]
x_train, x_test = x_train / 255.0, x_test
/ 255.0
```

2. **Build the Neural Network Model**: Next, define a simple neural network with an input layer, one hidden layer, and an output layer. Keras provides an easy-to-use `Sequential` model for defining a stack of layers.

    python

```
from       tensorflow.keras.models     import
Sequential
from       tensorflow.keras.layers     import
Flatten, Dense

# Build the model
model = Sequential([
    Flatten(input_shape=(28,    28)),     #
Flatten the 28x28 images into 1D vectors
    Dense(128,   activation='relu'),     #
Hidden  layer  with  128  neurons  and  ReLU
activation
    Dense(10,   activation='softmax')    #
Output  layer  with  10  neurons  (for  10
classes)
])
```

    In this model:

- o The **Flatten** layer converts each 28x28 image into a 1D vector of 784 values.
- o The **Dense** layer with 128 neurons and ReLU activation creates a fully connected layer.
- o The final **Dense** layer with 10 neurons corresponds to the 10 digit classes (0-9), and the softmax activation function is used to output probabilities.

3. **Compile the Model**: The model needs to be compiled before training. The compile() method specifies the optimizer, loss function, and evaluation metric:

```python
model.compile(optimizer='adam',

loss='sparse_categorical_crossentropy',   #
For multi-class classification
                metrics=['accuracy'])
```

- o **Adam** is a popular optimizer that adjusts learning rates based on the data and gradient.
- o **Sparse categorical crossentropy** is the loss function for multi-class classification tasks where the target labels are integers (instead of one-hot encoded).
- o **Accuracy** is used as the evaluation metric.

127

Training Neural Networks and Evaluating Performance

Once the model is compiled, we can train it using the training data. The `fit()` function trains the model for a specified number of epochs (iterations over the entire dataset).

1. **Training the Model**:

```python
# Train the model
model.fit(x_train, y_train, epochs=5)
```

In this example, the model will train for 5 epochs. During training, the model adjusts the weights using backpropagation to minimize the loss function.

2. **Evaluating the Model**: After training, we can evaluate the model on the test dataset to see how well it generalizes to unseen data.

```python
# Evaluate the model on the test data
test_loss,          test_acc          =
model.evaluate(x_test, y_test)
print(f'Test accuracy: {test_acc}')
```

128

The `evaluate()` function returns the loss and accuracy on the test set. The accuracy value is an indication of how well the model performs on the test data.

3. **Making Predictions**: After the model is trained, we can use it to make predictions on new data.

```python
# Make predictions on the test set
predictions = model.predict(x_test)

# Get the predicted class for each image
predicted_classes                          =
predictions.argmax(axis=1)
print(predicted_classes[:10])   # Show the
first 10 predictions
```

The `predict()` function returns the predicted probabilities for each class, and we use `argmax(axis=1)` to select the class with the highest probability as the predicted class.

Summary of Key Concepts:

- **Neural Networks**: A computational model inspired by the human brain that learns patterns in data.
- **Layers**: Neural networks consist of layers like input, hidden, and output layers.

- **Activation Functions**: Functions like ReLU, sigmoid, and softmax introduce non-linearity and help the network learn complex relationships.
- **Keras**: A high-level API in TensorFlow that simplifies building and training neural networks.
- **Training and Evaluation**: The model is trained using the `fit()` function, and performance is evaluated with `evaluate()`.

Real-World Example: Image Classification

In this chapter, we built a simple neural network to classify handwritten digits from the MNIST dataset. This is a classic example of how neural networks can be applied to image classification tasks. With TensorFlow and Keras, creating and training deep learning models is simplified, allowing you to focus on building the model and analyzing the results.

In the next chapter, we will explore **Convolutional Neural Networks (CNNs)**, which are specifically designed for image data and often perform significantly better than simple neural networks in tasks like image classification.

CHAPTER 13

CONVOLUTIONAL NEURAL NETWORKS (CNNS)

Understanding CNNs for Image Processing

Convolutional Neural Networks (CNNs) are a specialized type of deep learning model designed to handle grid-like data, such as images. Unlike traditional neural networks, which connect every neuron to every neuron in the next layer, CNNs are specifically designed to take advantage of the spatial structure of data, making them ideal for image recognition, object detection, and other computer vision tasks.

The primary advantage of CNNs lies in their ability to automatically detect patterns and features in images, such as edges, textures, and shapes, without requiring explicit feature extraction. This is achieved through the use of **convolutional layers** that apply filters to the image, capturing local patterns and spatial hierarchies.

CNNs consist of multiple layers that work together to process image data, with each layer learning different features. By stacking multiple convolutional and pooling layers, CNNs can learn hierarchical features, from simple edges in early layers to complex objects in deeper layers.

Layers in a CNN: Convolutional Layer, Pooling Layer, Fully Connected Layer

The architecture of a CNN typically includes the following layers:

1. **Convolutional Layer**:
   - o The core component of a CNN is the convolutional layer. This layer applies a set of filters (also called kernels) to the input image, sliding the filter over the image and computing the convolution operation at each position.
   - o The result of this operation is a feature map that represents the activations of different features detected by the filter.
   - o **Why Use Convolution?**: Convolution allows the model to capture local patterns (such as edges or textures) that are invariant to translation, meaning the model can detect the same feature regardless of its position in the image.

   Example: If you are processing an image of a cat, the convolutional layer might learn to detect features such as edges, fur patterns, or shapes like eyes and ears.

2. **Pooling Layer**:

- ○ Pooling layers reduce the spatial dimensions (width and height) of the feature maps while retaining the most important information. The most common pooling operation is **max pooling**, which selects the maximum value from a region of the feature map.
- ○ Pooling helps in reducing the computational complexity, prevents overfitting by providing an abstracted form of the data, and makes the model more invariant to small translations or distortions in the input image.

Example: If a feature map is of size 8x8, a 2x2 max pooling operation would reduce it to a 4x4 feature map, keeping the strongest features and discarding less important information.

3. **Fully Connected (Dense) Layer**:
- ○ The fully connected layer comes after the convolutional and pooling layers. It connects every neuron in the previous layer to every neuron in this layer, similar to a traditional neural network.
- ○ The fully connected layers are responsible for combining the features learned in the convolutional layers and making the final decision or prediction.

133

o In the case of image classification, the final fully connected layer typically outputs the class probabilities for each possible label (e.g., digits 0–9 in the MNIST dataset).

Example: In an image classification task, the fully connected layers combine features learned from the previous layers to predict the class (e.g., cat or dog).

Building a CNN for Image Classification

To build a Convolutional Neural Network (CNN) for image classification using TensorFlow and Keras, you typically follow these steps:

1. **Define the CNN architecture**: Stack convolutional layers, pooling layers, and fully connected layers.
2. **Compile the model**: Specify the optimizer, loss function, and evaluation metrics.
3. **Train the model**: Feed the model the training data and adjust the weights through backpropagation.
4. **Evaluate the model**: Test the model on unseen data to assess its generalization performance.

Here's a simple example of how to build and train a CNN for image classification using Keras:

Example: Building a CNN for Image Classification (MNIST Dataset)

1. **Loading the MNIST Dataset**: The MNIST dataset consists of 28x28 grayscale images of handwritten digits from 0 to 9. It is a standard dataset for image classification tasks.

python

```
from    tensorflow.keras.datasets    import
mnist

# Load the dataset
(x_train, y_train), (x_test, y_test) =
mnist.load_data()

# Normalize the images to values between 0
and 1
x_train, x_test = x_train / 255.0, x_test
/ 255.0

# Reshape the images to 28x28x1 (adding a
channel dimension for grayscale)
x_train = x_train.reshape(-1, 28, 28, 1)
x_test = x_test.reshape(-1, 28, 28, 1)
```

2. **Building the CNN Model**: Here, we will create a simple CNN with one convolutional layer, one pooling layer, and two fully connected layers.

```python
from tensorflow.keras import models, layers

# Initialize the CNN model
model = models.Sequential()

# Add a convolutional layer
model.add(layers.Conv2D(32, (3, 3), activation='relu', input_shape=(28, 28, 1)))

# Add a pooling layer
model.add(layers.MaxPooling2D((2, 2)))

# Flatten the output for the fully connected layer
model.add(layers.Flatten())

# Add a fully connected layer
model.add(layers.Dense(128, activation='relu'))
```

```
# Output layer with 10 neurons (one for
each digit) and softmax activation
model.add(layers.Dense(10,
activation='softmax'))
```

3. **Compiling the Model**: In this step, we choose an optimizer, a loss function, and evaluation metrics for the model. For a classification task like this, we use **categorical cross-entropy** as the loss function and **accuracy** as the metric.

```python
model.compile(optimizer='adam',

loss='sparse_categorical_crossentropy',
                metrics=['accuracy'])
```

4. **Training the Model**: We now train the model using the training data. The `fit()` function will adjust the weights of the network by minimizing the loss.

```python
model.fit(x_train,    y_train,    epochs=5,
batch_size=64)
```

The model will train for 5 epochs and update the weights after each batch.

5. **Evaluating the Model**: After training, we evaluate the model on the test set to determine how well it generalizes to unseen data.

```python
test_loss,              test_acc            =
model.evaluate(x_test, y_test)
print(f'Test accuracy: {test_acc}')
```

The test accuracy shows how well the model is performing on the test data that it hasn't seen before.

Real-World Example: Handwritten Digit Recognition (MNIST Dataset)

The MNIST dataset is a classic example for testing image classification algorithms, and it is often used as a benchmark for new models. By building a CNN, we were able to achieve high accuracy in classifying images of handwritten digits.

In this example, the CNN learns to recognize features such as edges, curves, and shapes that are characteristic of digits. By using convolutional and pooling layers, the network extracts increasingly complex features, while the fully connected layers at the end combine these features to make a final classification.

Once trained, the model can predict the digit in a new image. The ability of CNNs to handle image data makes them indispensable for tasks such as:

- **Medical image analysis** (e.g., detecting tumors in X-ray images),
- **Self-driving cars** (e.g., detecting pedestrians and objects),
- **Object recognition in images** (e.g., classifying images from social media).

Summary of Key Concepts:

- **CNNs**: Specialized neural networks designed for processing image data, with layers that detect spatial patterns.
- **Layers in a CNN**: Convolutional layers detect features, pooling layers reduce dimensionality, and fully connected layers make final predictions.
- **Activation Functions**: ReLU is commonly used in hidden layers to introduce non-linearity, and softmax is used in the output layer for multi-class classification.
- **Image Classification**: We used a simple CNN model to classify handwritten digits from the MNIST dataset, achieving high accuracy.

In the next chapter, we will explore **Recurrent Neural Networks (RNNs)**, which are specifically designed for sequence data, such as time series or natural language processing tasks.

CHAPTER 14

RECURRENT NEURAL NETWORKS (RNNS) AND LSTMS

What are Recurrent Neural Networks?

Recurrent Neural Networks (RNNs) are a type of neural network designed to handle sequential data. Unlike traditional feed-forward neural networks, RNNs have connections that form cycles, allowing them to maintain a **memory** of previous inputs in the sequence. This feature enables RNNs to learn and make predictions based on not just the current input but also the context provided by previous data points.

How RNNs Work:

- In a standard neural network, each input is processed independently. In contrast, RNNs process inputs sequentially, one step at a time, and use their previous hidden states (outputs) to influence the current step.

- At each time step, the RNN receives an input and produces an output. The hidden state of the RNN is updated at each step, maintaining memory of the previous inputs in the sequence.

RNN Formula: The core of an RNN can be mathematically represented as:

$$h_t = f(W \cdot x_t + U \cdot h_{t-1} + b)$$

Where:

- h_t is the hidden state at time step t,
- x_t is the input at time step t,
- h_{t-1} is the hidden state at the previous time step,
- W, U are the weights, and b is the bias.

The RNN updates the hidden state at each step, passing information along the sequence. However, traditional RNNs suffer from **vanishing gradient problems**, where the model struggles to retain information from long sequences during training. This leads to poor performance on tasks requiring long-term dependencies.

Long Short-Term Memory (LSTM) Networks

Long Short-Term Memory (LSTM) networks are a special kind of RNN that addresses the vanishing gradient problem and allows the model to retain information over longer sequences. LSTMs were introduced to improve the performance of RNNs by introducing

gates that control the flow of information into and out of the network.

LSTMs are designed to remember long-term dependencies by learning what to "remember" and what to "forget" at each time step. The three main components of an LSTM cell are:

1. **Forget Gate**: Decides what information should be discarded from the cell state.
2. **Input Gate**: Decides what new information should be added to the cell state.
3. **Output Gate**: Decides what part of the cell state should be outputted as the hidden state.

LSTM Architecture: The LSTM cell uses the following formulas to update its cell state and hidden state:

- Forget Gate:

  ft=σ(Wf·[ht−1,xt]+bf)f_t = \sigma(W_f \cdot [h_{t-1}, x_t] + b_f)ft=σ(Wf·[ht−1,xt]+bf)

- Input Gate:

  it=σ(Wi·[ht−1,xt]+bi)i_t = \sigma(W_i \cdot [h_{t-1}, x_t] + b_i)it=σ(Wi·[ht−1,xt]+bi)
  Ct~=tanh(WC·[ht−1,xt]+bC)\tilde{C_t} = \tanh(W_C \cdot [h_{t-1}, x_t] + b_C)Ct~=tanh(WC·[ht−1,xt]+bC)

- Cell State:

  Ct=ft*Ct−1+it*Ct~C_t = f_t * C_{t-1} + i_t * \tilde{C_t}Ct=ft*Ct−1+it*Ct~

- Output Gate:

  ot=σ(Wo·[ht−1,xt]+bo)o_t = \sigma(W_o \cdot [h_{t-1}, x_t] + b_o)ot=σ(Wo·[ht−1,xt]+bo) ht=ot*tanh(Ct)h_t = o_t * \tanh(C_t)ht=ot*tanh(Ct)

These gates allow the LSTM to selectively remember or forget information, making it particularly effective for tasks where long-term dependencies are important.

Applications of RNNs: Time Series Forecasting, Sentiment Analysis

RNNs and LSTMs are well-suited for tasks that involve sequential or time-dependent data. Some common applications include:

1. **Time Series Forecasting**: Time series data refers to data points collected or indexed in time order. Examples include stock prices, weather data, and sales trends. RNNs and LSTMs can be used to predict future values based on historical data by learning the temporal dependencies between observations.

Example: Predicting the next day's stock price based on the previous days' prices.

2. **Sentiment Analysis**: Sentiment analysis involves determining the sentiment (positive, negative, or neutral) of a given text. This is commonly applied to social media posts, reviews, or customer feedback. RNNs and LSTMs are well-suited for text processing because they can capture the order and dependencies between words in a sentence.

Example: Analyzing movie reviews to predict whether the sentiment is positive or negative.

3. **Speech Recognition**: RNNs are used in speech recognition systems to process sequences of audio features and map them to text.

4. **Machine Translation**: RNNs and LSTMs are used in neural machine translation systems, where the network learns to translate text from one language to another by processing sequential word representations.

Real-World Example: Predicting Stock Prices with RNN

Stock price prediction is a classic example of time series forecasting, where historical stock prices are used to predict future prices. Here, we'll use an LSTM model to predict the future closing prices of a stock based on its past closing prices.

145

1. **Load and Preprocess the Data**: The first step is to load historical stock price data. We'll use the Yahoo Finance API or another data source to retrieve the stock prices and preprocess the data.

```python
python

import pandas as pd
import numpy as np
from      sklearn.preprocessing      import
MinMaxScaler

# Load stock price data (use Yahoo Finance,
for example)
stock_data                             =
pd.read_csv('stock_prices.csv',
date_parser=True)
stock_data = stock_data[['Date', 'Close']]
# Only use date and closing price

# Normalize the data (important for LSTMs)
scaler  =  MinMaxScaler(feature_range=(0,
1))
stock_data['Close']                    =
scaler.fit_transform(stock_data[['Close']
])

# Prepare the data for training (e.g., last
60 days to predict the next day's price)
```

```
def create_dataset(data, time_step=60):
    X, y = [], []
    for i in range(len(data) - time_step -
1):
        X.append(data[i:(i + time_step),
0])
        y.append(data[i + time_step, 0])
    return np.array(X), np.array(y)

data                                      =
stock_data['Close'].values.reshape(-1, 1)
X, y = create_dataset(data)

# Reshape data for LSTM (samples, time
steps, features)
X = X.reshape(X.shape[0], X.shape[1], 1)
```

2. **Build the LSTM Model**: In this step, we define the architecture of the LSTM model. The model will consist of an LSTM layer followed by a dense output layer.

```
python
```

```
from    tensorflow.keras.models    import
Sequential
from tensorflow.keras.layers import LSTM,
Dense

# Define the model
```

```
model = Sequential()

# LSTM layer with 50 units and input shape
matching the data shape
model.add(LSTM(units=50,
return_sequences=False,
input_shape=(X.shape[1], 1)))

# Fully connected layer to output the
predicted stock price
model.add(Dense(units=1))

# Compile the model
model.compile(optimizer='adam',
loss='mean_squared_error')
```

3. **Train the Model**: We now train the model using the training data.

```python
# Train the model
model.fit(X, y, epochs=10, batch_size=32)
```

4. **Predict Future Stock Prices**: After training the model, we can use it to predict future stock prices.

```python
```

```
# Make predictions on the test data (or the
next day's price)
predictions = model.predict(X)

# Inverse transform predictions to original
scale
predictions                             =
scaler.inverse_transform(predictions)
```

5. **Evaluate the Model**: We can evaluate the model's performance by comparing predicted prices with actual prices using performance metrics like RMSE (Root Mean Squared Error).

```python
from        sklearn.metrics        import
mean_squared_error
rmse     =     np.sqrt(mean_squared_error(y,
predictions))
print(f'Root Mean Squared Error: {rmse}')
```

In this example, we used an LSTM model to predict the future closing prices of a stock based on its historical data. The model learns the temporal dependencies in the data, making it capable of predicting future prices.

Summary of Key Concepts:

- **Recurrent Neural Networks (RNNs)** are designed for sequential data, allowing the model to remember past inputs and use this information to make predictions.

- **LSTM (Long Short-Term Memory)** networks are a type of RNN designed to handle long-term dependencies by using gates to regulate information flow.

- **Applications of RNNs** include time series forecasting (e.g., stock price prediction), sentiment analysis, and machine translation.

- In the **real-world example**, we used an LSTM to predict stock prices based on historical data, demonstrating the power of RNNs in time series forecasting tasks.

In the next chapter, we will explore **Generative Adversarial Networks (GANs)**, which are used for generating new data samples, such as generating realistic images or music, based on learned patterns from existing data.

CHAPTER 15

NATURAL LANGUAGE PROCESSING (NLP)

Introduction to NLP

Natural Language Processing (NLP) is a subfield of artificial intelligence (AI) focused on the interaction between computers and human language. The goal of NLP is to enable computers to understand, interpret, and generate human language in a way that is meaningful and useful. NLP encompasses a variety of tasks, including text classification, sentiment analysis, machine translation, and speech recognition.

Key components of NLP:

- **Syntax**: The structure of sentences and how words are arranged.
- **Semantics**: The meaning of words and sentences.
- **Pragmatics**: The context in which language is used and how meaning is derived from this context.
- **Discourse**: How sentences and phrases interact in longer passages of text.

Applications of NLP include:

- **Chatbots and Virtual Assistants**: Systems that can understand and respond to user queries.
- **Sentiment Analysis**: Understanding the emotional tone behind a piece of text.
- **Machine Translation**: Translating text from one language to another.
- **Text Summarization**: Extracting the most important points from a text.

The goal of NLP is to bridge the gap between human communication and computer understanding, enabling machines to interact with humans in a more natural way.

Text Preprocessing: Tokenization, Lemmatization, Stemming

Before applying machine learning models to text data, it's essential to preprocess the text. Preprocessing involves preparing the text by breaking it down into smaller, manageable components and normalizing it for further analysis. The most common preprocessing techniques include tokenization, lemmatization, and stemming.

1. **Tokenization**: Tokenization is the process of breaking down a text into smaller units called tokens. Tokens are typically words, but they can also be characters or subwords. Tokenization helps to split the text into components that can be analyzed further.

152

Example:

```python
python

from nltk.tokenize import word_tokenize
text = "Natural language processing is
fun!"
tokens = word_tokenize(text)
print(tokens)
```

Output:

```
['Natural',    'language',    'processing',
'is', 'fun', '!']
```

2. **Lemmatization**: Lemmatization is the process of reducing words to their base or root form (called a lemma). Unlike stemming, which simply removes suffixes, lemmatization considers the word's meaning and returns the correct base form.

Example:

```python
python

from nltk.stem import WordNetLemmatizer
lemmatizer = WordNetLemmatizer()
word = "running"
lemma      =      lemmatizer.lemmatize(word,
pos='v')  # 'v' for verb
```

```
print(lemma)
```

Output:

```
'run'
```

Lemmatization ensures that words like "running", "runs", and "ran" are all reduced to the base form "run".

3. **Stemming**: Stemming is a simpler technique compared to lemmatization. It removes prefixes and suffixes from words to reduce them to a common stem. However, stemming may not always produce real words and can lead to loss of meaning.

Example:

```
python

from nltk.stem import PorterStemmer
stemmer = PorterStemmer()
word = "running"
stem = stemmer.stem(word)
print(stem)
```

Output:

```
'run'
```

Stemming reduces "running" to "run", but it may not always yield a valid word, as in the case of "better" being reduced to "better" (without meaning changes).

Bag of Words and TF-IDF

Once the text is tokenized and normalized, the next step is to convert the text data into a numerical representation that can be fed into machine learning models. Two common techniques for this are **Bag of Words (BoW)** and **TF-IDF (Term Frequency-Inverse Document Frequency)**.

1. **Bag of Words (BoW)**: The Bag of Words model represents text data as a collection of words and their frequencies. Each document is represented as a vector, with each element in the vector corresponding to the frequency of a specific word in the document. The order of the words is not preserved, meaning this model only considers word frequency.

   Example:

   ```python
   from sklearn.feature_extraction.text
   import CountVectorizer
   corpus = [
       "I love programming",
   ```

155

```
    "Programming is fun",
    "I love Python"
]
vectorizer = CountVectorizer()
X = vectorizer.fit_transform(corpus)
print(vectorizer.get_feature_names_out())
print(X.toarray())
```

Output:

```lua
['I',    'Python',    'Programming',    'is',
'love', 'fun']
[[1 0 1 0 1 0]
 [0 0 1 1 0 1]
 [1 1 0 0 1 0]]
```

Here, each document is represented as a vector with the frequency of words. For example, "I love programming" is represented by `[1, 0, 1, 0, 1, 0]`, meaning the word "I" appears once, "love" appears once, and "programming" appears once.

2. **TF-IDF (Term Frequency-Inverse Document Frequency)**: TF-IDF is an improvement over BoW, as it considers the importance of each word in the context of the entire corpus. It reduces the weight of words that appear frequently in many documents and increases the

156

weight of words that are rare but important for distinguishing between documents.

Formula:

- o **TF** (Term Frequency) measures how frequently a term occurs in a document.
- o **IDF** (Inverse Document Frequency) measures how important a term is in the entire corpus.

The TF-IDF score is calculated as:

TF-IDF(t,d)=TF(t,d)×IDF(t)\text{TF-IDF}(t, d) = \text{TF}(t, d) \times \text{IDF}(t)TF-IDF(t,d)=TF(t,d)×IDF(t)

Where:

- o ttt is the term,
- o ddd is the document,
- o TF(t,d)=Number of occurrences of term t in document dTotal number of terms in document d\text{TF}(t, d) = \frac{\text{Number of occurrences of term } t \text{ in document } d}{\text{Total number of terms in document } d}TF(t,d)=Total number of terms in document d Number of occurrences of term t in document d,

157

o IDF(t)=log⌈⁄₀⌉Total number of documentsNumber of documents containing term t\text{IDF}(t) = \log \frac{\text{Total number of documents}}{\text{Number of documents containing term }t}IDF(t)=logNumber of documents containing term tTotal number of documents.

Example:

```python
```

```
from        sklearn.feature_extraction.text
import TfidfVectorizer
corpus = [
    "I love programming",
    "Programming is fun",
    "I love Python"
]
vectorizer = TfidfVectorizer()
X = vectorizer.fit_transform(corpus)
print(vectorizer.get_feature_names_out())
print(X.toarray())
```

Output:

```lua
```

158

```
['I',    'Python',    'Programming',    'is',
'love', 'fun']
[[0.57735027 0.              0.57735027 0.
0.57735027 0.              ]
 [0.        0.             0.57735027 0.70710678
0.          0.70710678]
 [0.57735027 0.70710678 0.              0.
0.57735027 0.              ]]
```

Here, the vectors represent the **TF-IDF** values of words
in each document, capturing both the frequency and
importance of each word in the context of the entire
dataset.

Real-World Example: Sentiment Analysis on Social Media Posts

Sentiment analysis is a common NLP task where the goal is to
determine whether the sentiment of a piece of text is positive,
negative, or neutral. Social media platforms like Twitter or
Facebook provide a rich source of data for sentiment analysis. In
this example, we will use a simple approach to perform sentiment
analysis on social media posts using the **Bag of Words** model and
a classification algorithm.

1. **Collect and Preprocess the Data**: First, we gather social
    media posts, clean the text (tokenize, remove stopwords,
    etc.), and preprocess the text data.

    ```python
    python
    ```

```python
import pandas as pd
from sklearn.model_selection import train_test_split
from sklearn.feature_extraction.text import CountVectorizer

# Example social media posts and corresponding sentiments
data = pd.DataFrame({
    'text': ["I love this product!", "This is terrible, don't buy it!", "It's okay, but could be better.", "Amazing experience, highly recommend!"],
    'sentiment': [1, 0, 2, 1]   # 1: Positive, 0: Negative, 2: Neutral
})

# Preprocess the text data using CountVectorizer
vectorizer = CountVectorizer(stop_words='english')
X = vectorizer.fit_transform(data['text'])
y = data['sentiment']

# Split data into training and testing sets
X_train, X_test, y_train, y_test = train_test_split(X, y, test_size=0.2, random_state=42)
```

2. **Train a Sentiment Classifier**: We can train a machine learning classifier, such as **Logistic Regression**, to predict the sentiment of social media posts based on the Bag of Words features.

```python
from sklearn.linear_model import LogisticRegression
from sklearn.metrics import accuracy_score

# Initialize the model
model = LogisticRegression()

# Train the model
model.fit(X_train, y_train)

# Predict sentiment on test data
y_pred = model.predict(X_test)

# Evaluate the model
accuracy = accuracy_score(y_test, y_pred)
print(f'Accuracy: {accuracy}')
```

3. **Model Output**: The model predicts the sentiment of each social media post (positive, negative, or neutral). We can use various metrics (accuracy, precision, recall) to evaluate the model's performance.

161

Summary of Key Concepts:

- **Natural Language Processing (NLP)** enables computers to process and understand human language.
- **Text Preprocessing** techniques like **tokenization, stemming**, and **lemmatization** prepare the text for further analysis.
- **Bag of Words** and **TF-IDF** are used to convert text data into numerical vectors for machine learning models.
- **Sentiment Analysis** is a common NLP application, and we've demonstrated how to perform sentiment analysis on social media posts.

In the next chapter, we will explore **Transformers and Attention Mechanisms**, which are the backbone of state-of-the-art NLP models like BERT and GPT. These models have revolutionized NLP by allowing for more sophisticated understanding of language context and relationships.

CHAPTER 16

TRANSFORMERS AND ATTENTION MECHANISMS

What is a Transformer Model?

The **Transformer model** has revolutionized the field of Natural Language Processing (NLP) and is the foundation for most modern state-of-the-art models, including BERT and GPT. Introduced in the paper *"Attention Is All You Need"* by Vaswani et al. in 2017, the Transformer model addresses the limitations of traditional sequential models like Recurrent Neural Networks (RNNs) and Long Short-Term Memory (LSTM) networks.

The key innovation of the Transformer is its ability to process input data in **parallel** rather than sequentially, significantly speeding up training and allowing it to capture long-range dependencies in the data. The Transformer model is based on an **encoder-decoder** architecture, making it versatile for tasks like machine translation, text generation, and more.

Key Components of the Transformer:

1. **Self-Attention**: Allows the model to weigh the importance of different words in the input sequence, capturing relationships between distant words.

163

2. **Positional Encoding**: Since Transformers process the entire sequence in parallel, positional encoding is used to inject information about the order of words into the model.

3. **Encoder-Decoder Architecture**: The encoder processes the input sequence and generates hidden states, which are then passed to the decoder to produce the output sequence.

Transformers are highly parallelizable, making them faster to train and more efficient than RNNs and LSTMs, especially for large datasets and long sequences.

Attention Mechanisms and Self-Attention

At the heart of the Transformer model is the **attention mechanism**, which allows the model to focus on specific parts of the input sequence when making predictions. Traditional neural networks treat all inputs equally, but attention mechanisms help the model decide which parts of the sequence are most relevant for the current task.

1. **Attention Mechanism**:
    o The attention mechanism computes a weighted sum of the input sequence, where the weights are learned dynamically based on the input itself.

- o It helps the model to "attend" to different parts of the sequence depending on the context, which is particularly useful for tasks where dependencies exist between distant words in the sequence.

Formula for Attention: The attention mechanism uses three vectors: **Query (Q)**, **Key (K)**, and **Value (V)**. The output of the attention mechanism is a weighted sum of the values (V), where the weights are determined by the similarity between the query and key.

Attention(Q,K,V)=softmax(QKTdk)V\text{Attention}(Q , K, V) = \text{softmax}\left(\frac{QK^T}{\sqrt{d_k}}\right) VAttention(Q,K,V)=softmax(dkQKT)V

Where:

- o QQQ is the query vector (representing the current word),
- o KKK is the key vector (representing all words in the sequence),
- o VVV is the value vector (containing the information to be passed along),
- o dkd_kdk is the dimension of the key vector (used for scaling).

2. **Self-Attention**:

- o Self-attention is a special case of attention where the query, key, and value all come from the same sequence of words. This means each word in the sequence attends to every other word in the sequence, allowing the model to capture relationships between distant words.
- o Self-attention is particularly effective for tasks like machine translation, where the meaning of a word can depend on words from far earlier in the sequence.

Example of Self-Attention: If we have the sentence "The cat sat on the mat," the word "cat" will attend to "the" (in "the cat") and "sat" (in "sat on the mat"), allowing the model to understand the context better.

BERT and GPT Models

BERT (Bidirectional Encoder Representations from Transformers) and **GPT (Generative Pretrained Transformer)** are two groundbreaking models based on the Transformer architecture, each excelling in different aspects of NLP.

1. **BERT**:
   - o BERT is a **pretrained language model** that learns bidirectional representations of text.

Unlike previous models that read text from left to right or right to left, BERT reads the entire sequence at once, capturing context from both directions simultaneously. This allows it to understand the full context of each word in a sentence.

o BERT is designed for tasks that involve understanding the meaning of a given piece of text, such as question answering, named entity recognition, and sentence classification.

BERT Training: BERT is pretrained on a large corpus of text using **masked language modeling** and **next sentence prediction** tasks:

o **Masked Language Modeling**: Randomly masks words in the input sequence and trains the model to predict them based on the surrounding context.

o **Next Sentence Prediction**: Trains the model to predict whether two sentences are sequential in a text corpus.

2. **GPT**:

o GPT is a **generative model** that excels in generating text based on a given input. Unlike BERT, which is designed for understanding tasks, GPT is trained to predict the next word in a sequence, making it ideal for text generation tasks.

o   GPT uses **unidirectional** (left-to-right) context, meaning it only considers the words that come before the current word when generating the next word.

o   GPT has been fine-tuned for a wide range of applications, including text generation, translation, and summarization.

GPT-3: GPT-3, the third version of the GPT series, is one of the largest language models ever created, with 175 billion parameters. It can generate highly coherent and contextually appropriate text across a wide variety of topics, and has shown remarkable capabilities in tasks such as answering questions, writing essays, and even coding.

Real-World Example: Text Generation with GPT-3

GPT-3 is a powerful tool for generating human-like text. Given a prompt, GPT-3 can generate coherent and contextually relevant text that flows naturally. Below is an example of how GPT-3 can be used for text generation.

1.   **Using GPT-3 for Text Generation**: GPT-3 can be accessed via the OpenAI API. To generate text, you

simply send a prompt to the API, and it will return the generated continuation of the text.

Example use case: **Generating a short story**:

```python
import openai

# Set your OpenAI API key
openai.api_key = "your-api-key"

# Define the prompt
prompt = "Once upon a time in a distant galaxy, there was a planet full of curious creatures. One day, a young creature named Zora decided to embark on an adventure."

# Generate the text
response = openai.Completion.create(
    engine="text-davinci-003",    # GPT-3 engine
    prompt=prompt,
    max_tokens=200,  # Limit the number of tokens (words)
    temperature=0.7,           # Controls randomness of the output (0.0 to 1.0)
    n=1,  # Number of responses to generate
```

```
        stop=None   # Define a stopping point
for generation
)


# Print the generated text
print(response.choices[0].text)
```

Example Output:

```vbnet
Zora's journey began with a long trek
across the purple hills of her home planet.
She had heard stories about the great
mountain where the stars met the earth, and
she was determined to find it. Along the
way, she encountered strange creatures and
learned many lessons about bravery and
curiosity. By the time she reached the
mountain, she had become not only a skilled
adventurer but also a wise and thoughtful
leader. And as the stars shimmered above
her, she realized that her adventure was
just beginning...
```

In this example, GPT-3 generates a continuation of the story based on the prompt. It maintains coherence and creativity, producing high-quality text.

Key Takeaways:

- **Transformers** are a revolutionary architecture that enables deep learning models to process sequences in parallel, capturing long-range dependencies through self-attention.
- **Attention mechanisms** allow models to focus on specific parts of the input sequence, making them more effective at tasks like translation, summarization, and text generation.
- **BERT** is a powerful bidirectional model for understanding the context of text, while **GPT** is a unidirectional model that excels in text generation.
- **GPT-3** can generate highly coherent and contextually relevant text, making it useful for applications like creative writing, conversation generation, and more.

In the next chapter, we will explore **Reinforcement Learning**, where we will dive into how agents learn by interacting with their environment and receiving feedback to maximize rewards.

CHAPTER 17

REINFORCEMENT LEARNING: TRAINING AGENTS

What is Reinforcement Learning?

Reinforcement Learning (RL) is a type of machine learning where an agent learns to make decisions by interacting with an environment. Unlike supervised learning, where the model is trained on labeled data, in RL, the agent learns through trial and error by receiving feedback in the form of rewards or penalties.

The goal of reinforcement learning is to find an optimal policy, which is a strategy for choosing actions that maximize the long-term cumulative reward. RL has applications in various fields, such as robotics, game playing, autonomous vehicles, and recommendation systems.

The key idea is that an agent takes actions in an environment, observes the results of those actions (in the form of a state and reward), and adjusts its behavior to maximize the total reward over time.

Components of a Reinforcement Learning Problem

Reinforcement learning problems consist of several key components that define how an agent learns to interact with its environment:

1. **Agent**:
   - The learner or decision-maker that interacts with the environment. The agent chooses actions based on its observations of the environment.

2. **Environment**:
   - The system with which the agent interacts. The environment responds to the agent's actions by providing new states and rewards.

3. **State**:
   - A representation of the environment at a specific point in time. States describe the current situation of the agent in the environment.
   - For example, in a game, the state could be the current configuration of the board or the position of the player.

4. **Action**:
   - The decisions or moves that the agent can make. The set of all possible actions is called the **action space**.
   - For example, in a chess game, the actions are the legal moves a player can make.

5. **Reward**:
   o A scalar feedback signal that indicates the immediate benefit of the action taken by the agent. The reward can be positive (reward) or negative (penalty).
   o For example, in a game, a win may yield a positive reward, while a loss could result in a negative reward.

6. **Policy**:
   o A policy is a strategy that defines the agent's behavior. It maps from states to actions, guiding the agent on what action to take in any given state.
   o The goal of RL is to learn the **optimal policy**, which maximizes the cumulative reward.

7. **Value Function**:
   o The value function estimates the long-term reward an agent can expect to accumulate starting from a particular state or state-action pair. It helps the agent evaluate which states are more "valuable" in terms of future rewards.

8. **Discount Factor** (γ\gamma$\gamma$):
   o The discount factor determines how much future rewards are valued compared to immediate rewards. A discount factor close to 1 means future rewards are highly valued, while a value close to

0 means the agent is more focused on immediate rewards.

Markov Decision Processes (MDPs)

A **Markov Decision Process (MDP)** is a mathematical framework used to model reinforcement learning problems. MDPs describe the dynamics of the environment, the agent's decision-making process, and the rewards. An MDP is defined by the following components:

1. **States (S)**: The set of all possible states the environment can be in.
2. **Actions (A)**: The set of all possible actions the agent can take.
3. **Transition Function (T)**: A function that defines the probability of transitioning from one state to another given an action. The transition function is often written as $P(s'|s,a)P(s' \mid s, a)P(s'|s,a)$, where $s's's'$ is the next state, sss is the current state, and aaa is the action taken.
4. **Reward Function (R)**: A function that defines the immediate reward the agent receives after taking an action in a given state, denoted as $R(s,a)R(s, a)R(s,a)$.
5. **Discount Factor (γ\gamma$\gamma$)**: A value between 0 and 1 that determines the importance of future rewards compared to immediate rewards. A higher value of γ\gamma$\gamma$ means future rewards are more important.

In an MDP, the goal is to find an optimal policy that maximizes the expected sum of rewards over time, taking into account both immediate and future rewards.

Solving an MDP: Value Iteration and Policy Iteration

To solve an MDP, we often use **Value Iteration** or **Policy Iteration** algorithms:

- **Value Iteration**: Iteratively updates the value of each state based on the rewards and transitions, and eventually converges to the optimal value function.
- **Policy Iteration**: Alternates between evaluating the current policy and improving it until the optimal policy is found.

Real-World Example: Building a Game Agent (e.g., Tic-Tac-Toe)

One of the most straightforward applications of reinforcement learning is in game playing. Let's consider building an agent to play the game **Tic-Tac-Toe** using reinforcement learning.

1. **State Representation**: The state in Tic-Tac-Toe can be represented as a 3x3 grid, where each cell can be either "X", "O", or empty. The state is the current configuration of the board.

176

2. **Action Representation**: The actions are the available moves the agent can make. At each step, the agent can choose to place "X" in any of the available empty spaces.

3. **Reward Function**:
   - The agent receives a positive reward (e.g., +1) if it wins the game.
   - The agent receives a negative reward (e.g., -1) if it loses.
   - The agent receives a neutral reward (e.g., 0) for a draw or non-terminal state.

4. **Policy**: The agent learns a policy that guides it to take the best actions to maximize its chances of winning, based on its current state.

5. **Training the Agent**: We can use **Q-Learning**, a model-free reinforcement learning algorithm, to train the agent. Q-Learning updates a **Q-table** that estimates the value of each state-action pair. The Q-value is updated based on the reward received and the maximum future Q-value.

Q-Learning Algorithm:

1. Initialize the Q-table with zeros.
2. At each state, the agent selects an action based on an **exploration-exploitation** strategy (e.g., epsilon-greedy).
3. The agent takes the action, receives a reward, and transitions to a new state.
4. The Q-value is updated using the formula:

$$Q(s,a)=Q(s,a)+\alpha(R(s,a)+\gamma\max_{a'}Q(s',a')-Q(s,a))Q(s, a)$$
$$= Q(s, a) + \alpha \left(R(s, a) + \gamma \max_{a'} Q(s', a') - Q(s, a) \right)Q(s,a)=Q(s,a)+\alpha(R(s,a)+\gamma a'\max Q(s',a')-Q(s,a))$$

Where:

- $Q(s,a)Q(s, a)Q(s,a)$ is the Q-value of the state-action pair,
- $R(s,a)R(s, a)R(s,a)$ is the reward for taking action aaa in state sss,
- $\max_{a'}Q(s',a')\max_{a'} Q(s', a')\max a'Q(s',a')$ is the maximum Q-value for the next state $s's's'$,
- $\alpha\alpha\alpha$ is the learning rate,
- $\gamma\gamma\gamma$ is the discount factor.

Example Code for Tic-Tac-Toe Agent:

python

```python
import random

class TicTacToeAgent:
    def __init__(self, alpha=0.5, gamma=0.9, epsilon=0.1):
        self.alpha = alpha  # Learning rate
        self.gamma = gamma  # Discount factor
        self.epsilon = epsilon  # Exploration rate
```

```
        self.q_table = {}   # Q-table to store
state-action values

    def get_state(self, board):
        # Convert board to a tuple for hashable
state representation
        return tuple(board)


    def         choose_action(self,          state,
available_actions):
        # Epsilon-greedy strategy
        if random.uniform(0, 1) < self.epsilon:
            return
random.choice(available_actions)   # Explore
        else:
            # Exploit: Choose the action with the
highest Q-value
            q_values = [self.q_table.get((state,
action), 0) for action in available_actions]
            max_q_value = max(q_values)
            best_actions = [action for action,
q_value in zip(available_actions, q_values) if
q_value == max_q_value]
            return random.choice(best_actions)


    def update_q_table(self,   state,   action,
reward, next_state, next_available_actions):
        # Update Q-value using the Q-Learning
formula
```

179

```
        max_future_q                    =
max([self.q_table.get((next_state, a), 0) for a
in next_available_actions])
        current_q   =   self.q_table.get((state,
action), 0)
        self.q_table[(state,      action)]      =
current_q + self.alpha * (reward + self.gamma *
max_future_q - current_q)
```

In this example, the agent uses Q-Learning to improve its gameplay by updating its Q-values during each game. The choose_action method uses an epsilon-greedy strategy to balance exploration and exploitation. Over time, the agent learns to maximize its expected reward by playing optimal moves.

Key Takeaways:

- **Reinforcement Learning (RL)** enables agents to learn through interaction with the environment by maximizing cumulative rewards.
- **Components of RL** include the agent, environment, states, actions, rewards, policy, and value functions.
- **Markov Decision Processes (MDPs)** provide a framework to model decision-making problems in RL.
- **Q-Learning** is a model-free RL algorithm used to learn the optimal policy without a model of the environment.

180

- **Real-World Example**: In the Tic-Tac-Toe example, the agent learns the optimal moves through trial and error using Q-Learning.

In the next chapter, we will dive into **Deep Reinforcement Learning**, which combines neural networks with RL to tackle more complex problems, such as playing video games and robotic control.

CHAPTER 18

EVALUATION OF DEEP LEARNING MODELS

Evaluating Deep Learning Models: Loss Functions, Accuracy

Evaluating the performance of deep learning models is a critical step in ensuring that the model learns correctly and generalizes well to unseen data. The evaluation involves checking how well the model performs both during training and after it has been deployed for testing.

1. **Loss Functions**:
    o   A **loss function** (also known as a cost function) measures the difference between the predicted output of the model and the actual target values. The goal of training is to minimize the loss function, which means the model's predictions are as close as possible to the actual targets.
    o   Different types of loss functions are used depending on the nature of the task:
        ▪   **Mean Squared Error (MSE)**: Used for regression tasks where the target variable is continuous. It measures the average of

the squared differences between predicted and actual values.

- **Cross-Entropy Loss**: Used for classification tasks. It measures the performance of a classification model whose output is a probability value between 0 and 1. For binary classification, it's also known as **binary cross-entropy**, and for multi-class classification, it's **categorical cross-entropy**.

Example for Regression (MSE):

python

```
from     tensorflow.keras.losses     import
MeanSquaredError
loss_fn = MeanSquaredError()
loss_value = loss_fn(y_true, y_pred)
```

Example for Classification (Categorical Cross-Entropy):

python

```
from     tensorflow.keras.losses     import
CategoricalCrossentropy
loss_fn = CategoricalCrossentropy()
```

```
loss_value = loss_fn(y_true, y_pred)
```

2. **Accuracy**:

   o **Accuracy** is a simple and widely used evaluation metric for classification problems. It measures the percentage of correct predictions made by the model. However, accuracy alone may not always be sufficient, especially when dealing with imbalanced datasets.

   Formula for accuracy:

   Accuracy=Number of Correct PredictionsTotal Number of Predictions\text{Accuracy} = \frac{\text{Number of Correct Predictions}}{\text{Total Number of Predictions}}Accuracy=Total Number of PredictionsNumber of Correct Predictions

   In Keras, accuracy can be easily computed as follows:

```python
from tensorflow.keras.metrics import Accuracy
accuracy_fn = Accuracy()
accuracy_value = accuracy_fn(y_true, y_pred)
```

For **binary classification**, the **binary accuracy** metric is used, and for **multi-class classification**, the **categorical accuracy** is used.

Training Deep Models: Epochs, Batch Size

When training deep learning models, the data is often large and cannot be processed all at once. Therefore, the data is divided into smaller **batches**, and the model is trained over multiple **epochs**.

1. **Epochs**:
   - An **epoch** is one complete pass through the entire training dataset. During each epoch, the model updates its weights based on the data and the loss function. More epochs allow the model to learn more from the data, but too many epochs can lead to **overfitting**, where the model performs well on training data but poorly on unseen data.

   Choosing the number of epochs:

   - A typical approach is to use cross-validation to find the optimal number of epochs. You can monitor the validation loss during training to check for overfitting and stop training early when performance on the validation set starts to degrade.

185

Example:

```python
```

```python
model.fit(X_train, y_train, epochs=10,
validation_data=(X_val, y_val))
```

2. **Batch Size**:

   o **Batch size** is the number of training samples used in one forward and backward pass through the network. Instead of updating weights after each individual training sample (stochastic gradient descent), or after all the data (batch gradient descent), **mini-batch gradient descent** updates the weights after a fixed number of samples (the batch size).

The choice of batch size affects the training process:

   o **Small batch sizes**: Offer more frequent updates, which can help avoid local minima but can be noisy.
   o **Large batch sizes**: Provide more stable estimates of the gradients but can be slower and more prone to overfitting.

Typical batch sizes are powers of 2 (e.g., 32, 64, 128).

186

Example:

```python
model.fit(X_train, y_train, batch_size=32,
epochs=10)
```

Challenges in Deep Learning: Exploding and Vanishing Gradients

Training deep learning models, especially very deep networks, presents several challenges, two of the most common being **exploding gradients** and **vanishing gradients**. Both problems are related to how gradients are propagated back through the network during training.

1. **Vanishing Gradients**:
    o The **vanishing gradient problem** occurs when the gradients (the partial derivatives of the loss function with respect to the weights) become very small as they are propagated backward through the network. This can happen when activation functions like **sigmoid** or **tanh** squash the output into a narrow range, leading to very small gradients.
    o When the gradients are too small, the model's weights are not updated significantly, and the

187

network stops learning, especially in the lower layers.

Solution: Use activation functions like **ReLU**, which are less likely to cause the vanishing gradient problem because they do not squash the input into a narrow range.

2. **Exploding Gradients**:
   o The **exploding gradient problem** occurs when the gradients become very large during backpropagation. This can cause the model's weights to become very large, leading to unstable training and potentially causing the model to diverge.
   o This often happens in deep networks or when using large learning rates.

Solution: Techniques like **gradient clipping** (setting a threshold for gradients) can prevent gradients from growing too large.

Example of Gradient Clipping:

```python
from tensorflow.keras.optimizers import Adam
```

```
optimizer = Adam(clipvalue=1.0)    # Clip
gradients to a maximum value of 1.0
model.compile(optimizer=optimizer,
loss='categorical_crossentropy')
```

Using Dropout and Batch Normalization

To mitigate some of the challenges in training deep learning models, two techniques—**dropout** and **batch normalization**—are commonly used to improve model generalization and accelerate convergence.

1. **Dropout**:
    o **Dropout** is a regularization technique that helps prevent overfitting by randomly setting a fraction of the input units to zero during training. This prevents the model from becoming too reliant on certain neurons and forces it to learn more robust features.
    o Dropout is usually applied to the fully connected layers of the network.

Example:

```
python
```

```
from tensorflow.keras.layers import Dropout
```

189

```
model.add(Dense(128, activation='relu'))
model.add(Dropout(0.5))    # 50% of the
neurons are dropped out during training
```

In this example, 50% of the neurons in the fully connected layer are randomly dropped out during training, which helps prevent the model from overfitting.

2. **Batch Normalization**:
   o **Batch normalization** is a technique used to normalize the activations of each layer in the network. This helps to reduce internal covariate shift, accelerates training, and improves the model's performance.
   o Batch normalization is usually applied before the activation function.

Example:

```
python
```

```
from    tensorflow.keras.layers    import
BatchNormalization

model.add(Dense(128))
model.add(BatchNormalization())              #
Normalize the layer's output
model.add(Activation('relu'))
```

Batch normalization adjusts the output of each layer by normalizing it across the mini-batch and then scaling and shifting it with learnable parameters. This helps the model converge faster and often leads to better performance.

Key Takeaways:

- **Loss Functions** and **Accuracy** are crucial for evaluating the performance of deep learning models.
- **Epochs** and **Batch Size** control the training process, with careful tuning required to balance training time and model performance.
- **Exploding** and **Vanishing Gradients** are common challenges in deep networks, and techniques like **ReLU activation** and **gradient clipping** can help address them.
- **Dropout** and **Batch Normalization** are regularization techniques that help improve model generalization, reduce overfitting, and accelerate training.

In the next chapter, we will explore **Transfer Learning**, a technique that leverages pre-trained models to solve new tasks with minimal data and training.

CHAPTER 19

INTRODUCTION TO MODEL DEPLOYMENT

What is Model Deployment?

Model deployment is the process of taking a machine learning model that has been trained and tested, and making it available for use in real-world applications. It involves integrating the model into a production environment where it can make predictions on new, incoming data. Model deployment is a crucial step in the machine learning lifecycle, as it allows the model to be used by end-users or other systems for real-time decision-making, automation, and business intelligence.

The deployment process typically involves several stages, including:

1. **Model Serialization**: Saving the trained model in a format that can be loaded and used later (e.g., `.pkl`, `.h5` for Keras models).
2. **Building an API**: Exposing the model through a web service that can handle incoming requests and provide predictions.

3. **Cloud Deployment**: Deploying the model to a cloud platform like AWS, Google Cloud, or Azure to make it scalable and accessible from anywhere.

4. **Monitoring and Maintenance**: After deployment, continuous monitoring is required to ensure the model is performing as expected and to retrain it when necessary.

Effective deployment ensures that the model can make accurate predictions on new data, scale as needed, and be maintained over time.

Setting Up APIs with Flask/Django

One of the most common ways to deploy a machine learning model is by setting up an API (Application Programming Interface) that serves the model. APIs allow external applications or users to interact with the model via HTTP requests and receive predictions in response.

Two popular Python frameworks for building APIs are **Flask** and **Django**. Both are lightweight web frameworks that enable you to create RESTful APIs easily.

1. **Flask**:
    o **Flask** is a lightweight micro-framework for Python that is great for small to medium-sized applications. It is widely used to expose machine

learning models through APIs because of its simplicity.

o Flask allows you to set up routes that handle requests and return model predictions.

Example of API with Flask: Here's how to deploy a simple model using Flask:

```python

from flask import Flask, request, jsonify
import numpy as np
import pickle

# Initialize Flask app
app = Flask(__name__)

# Load the trained machine learning model
model = pickle.load(open('model.pkl', 'rb'))

# Define API endpoint for prediction
@app.route('/predict', methods=['POST'])
def predict():
    try:
        # Get input data from the request
        data = request.get_json()
        # Convert input data to a numpy array
```

194

```
        features                        =
np.array(data['features']).reshape(1, -1)
        # Make prediction
        prediction                      =
model.predict(features)
        # Return the result as JSON
        return       jsonify({'prediction':
prediction.tolist()})
    except Exception as e:
        return jsonify({'error': str(e)})

# Run the Flask app
if __name__ == '__main__':
    app.run(debug=True)
```

In this example, we load a trained model from a file (model.pkl) and set up a /predict endpoint that accepts POST requests with input features. The model makes predictions based on the input data, and the result is returned in JSON format.

To test the API, you can send a POST request using a tool like **Postman** or by making HTTP requests with Python's requests library:

```python

import requests
```

```
url = 'http://localhost:5000/predict'
data = {'features': [5.1, 3.5, 1.4, 0.2]}
# Example input for a model
response = requests.post(url, json=data)
print(response.json())
```

2. **Django**:

   o **Django** is a more feature-rich framework compared to Flask. It is great for larger applications that require features such as authentication, database integration, and admin interfaces.

   o Django can also be used to deploy machine learning models, though it is generally more complex than Flask.

Basic Setup with Django: For deploying models with Django, you would typically follow these steps:

   o Create a Django project and app.
   o Set up views that handle HTTP requests and use your trained model to make predictions.
   o Expose your predictions through Django URLs (URLs are analogous to Flask routes).

Django is best used when you need to build a more robust application with additional features beyond just the API layer.

Deploying a Machine Learning Model to the Cloud (e.g., AWS, Google Cloud)

Once you have developed an API, the next step is to deploy your machine learning model to the cloud to ensure that it is scalable and accessible from anywhere. Cloud platforms like **AWS**, **Google Cloud**, and **Microsoft Azure** provide various services to help deploy machine learning models efficiently.

1. **Deploying to AWS**: AWS offers services like **Amazon SageMaker** and **AWS Lambda** for deploying machine learning models.

    o **Amazon SageMaker**: A fully managed service that provides an end-to-end solution for training, deploying, and scaling machine learning models. With SageMaker, you can deploy your model in a matter of minutes with minimal setup.

    o **AWS Lambda**: A serverless computing service that lets you deploy models without managing servers. You can use Lambda to create APIs that trigger machine learning predictions.

    Steps for deploying to AWS Lambda:

    o Package your model and dependencies into a zip file.

197

o Create an AWS Lambda function and upload the zip file.

o Set up an API Gateway to expose the Lambda function as an HTTP endpoint.

Example: You can upload the model and script to Lambda and use API Gateway to expose the model via an endpoint for prediction requests.

2. **Deploying to Google Cloud**: Google Cloud provides **AI Platform** and **Cloud Functions** to deploy models.

o **Google AI Platform**: A fully managed service for training, deploying, and serving machine learning models. It supports popular frameworks like TensorFlow, PyTorch, and Scikit-learn.

o **Google Cloud Functions**: A serverless platform for deploying lightweight functions that can respond to HTTP requests. This can be useful for creating simple prediction APIs.

Steps for deploying to Google Cloud:

o Train your model and save it (e.g., as a `.pkl` or `.h5` file).

o Use Google AI Platform to deploy the model.

o Expose the model via an HTTP API endpoint for predictions.

198

Serving Models in Production

Once a machine learning model is deployed, it is important to ensure that it works well in production. Serving models involves making predictions in real-time and handling various challenges that arise in production environments.

1. **Model Versioning**:
   - As your model improves over time (e.g., after retraining), it is important to keep track of different versions of the model. This allows you to manage deployments and roll back to previous versions if needed.

2. **Monitoring**:
   - After deployment, you should monitor the model's performance to ensure it continues to produce accurate results. This includes tracking metrics such as prediction latency, error rates, and resource usage.
   - You can use tools like **Prometheus** or **Grafana** for monitoring, or leverage built-in monitoring features from cloud platforms.

3. **Scaling**:
   - As the number of requests to the API grows, you may need to scale the system to handle increased traffic. This can be done by:

199

- **Horizontal scaling**: Adding more instances of the model to distribute the load.
- **Vertical scaling**: Increasing the computational resources of the current instance.

4. **Continuous Integration and Continuous Deployment (CI/CD)**:

   o For ongoing improvements, it is important to set up a **CI/CD pipeline** that automates the process of model retraining, testing, and deployment. This ensures that updates to the model can be quickly and safely deployed to production.

Key Takeaways:

- **Model Deployment** is the process of making a machine learning model available for real-world use, and it is a crucial step in the machine learning lifecycle.
- **APIs** can be built with frameworks like **Flask** and **Django** to expose models and make predictions through HTTP requests.
- **Cloud Deployment** with platforms like **AWS** and **Google Cloud** allows for scalable, production-ready deployment of machine learning models.

200

- **Serving Models in Production** involves ensuring the model works efficiently, scaling the infrastructure, and monitoring performance.

In the next chapter, we will dive into **Model Monitoring and Maintenance**, focusing on how to track the performance of models in production and manage model drift, ensuring that your model continues to deliver accurate results over time.

CHAPTER 20

ADVANCED DEEP LEARNING: GENERATIVE MODELS

What are Generative Models?

Generative models are a class of machine learning models that are designed to generate new data points that are similar to the data they were trained on. Unlike traditional discriminative models that predict a label or class for given input data (e.g., classification tasks), generative models learn the underlying distribution of the data and can generate new instances that resemble the original data distribution.

For example, a generative model trained on images of cats can create new, never-seen-before images of cats. These models are useful in various applications, such as:

- **Data augmentation**: Generating new samples from existing data to improve model training.
- **Creative content generation**: Producing realistic images, music, or text.
- **Simulating realistic environments**: Creating environments for training other machine learning models (e.g., robots or autonomous vehicles).

Generative models are typically based on probability theory and aim to model the data distribution $P(x)P(x)P(x)$, where xxx represents a data point. They can be categorized into different types, such as **variational autoencoders (VAEs)**, **generative adversarial networks (GANs)**, and **normalizing flows**.

Generative Adversarial Networks (GANs)

Generative Adversarial Networks (GANs) are one of the most powerful and popular types of generative models. GANs consist of two neural networks that are trained simultaneously through a process of competition:

1. **The Generator (G)**: The generator's job is to create fake data that looks as realistic as possible. It takes random noise as input and tries to generate data points that resemble real data.

2. **The Discriminator (D)**: The discriminator's job is to distinguish between real data (from the training set) and fake data (generated by the generator). It outputs a probability indicating whether a given input is real or fake.

The two networks are trained together in a **zero-sum game** where the generator tries to fool the discriminator, and the discriminator tries to correctly identify whether the data is real or fake. Over time, the generator improves at producing realistic data, and the discriminator becomes better at distinguishing real from fake data.

This adversarial process drives both models to improve their performance until the generator produces data indistinguishable from the real data.

GAN Training:

- The generator and discriminator are trained iteratively. The generator is updated based on how well it fools the discriminator, while the discriminator is updated to improve its ability to distinguish real from fake.

- The **objective function** for training a GAN is based on minimizing the loss of the discriminator and maximizing the loss of the generator, as follows:

$L(D,G)=Ex{\sim}Pdata(x)[\log f_0 D(x)]+Ez{\sim}Pz(z)[\log f_0 (1-D(G(z)))]L(D, G) = \mathbb{E}_{x \sim P_{\text{data}}(x)}[\log D(x)] + \mathbb{E}_{z \sim P_{\text{z}}(z)}[\log(1 - D(G(z)))]L(D,G)=Ex{\sim}Pdata(x)[\log D(x)]+Ez{\sim}Pz(z)[\log(1-D(G(z)))]$

Where:

- $D(x)D(x)D(x)$ is the probability that the discriminator believes xxx is real.

204

o $G(z)G(z)G(z)$ is the output of the generator when given random noise zzz.

The training process continues until the generator produces data so realistic that the discriminator can no longer reliably tell the difference.

Example of GAN Architecture:

sql

```
+------------+          +------------+          +-
--------------+
|   Noise    | ---->   | Generator  | ---->  |
Generated Data |
+------------+          +------------+          +-
--------------+
       ^
       |
       v
+------------+          +------------+
|  Real Data | ---->   | Discriminator|
+------------+          +------------+
```

In this architecture:

- **Noise** is random input to the generator.
- The **Generator** creates fake data based on the noise.

- The **Discriminator** evaluates the data and determines whether it's real or fake.

Applications of GANs: Image Synthesis, Style Transfer

Generative Adversarial Networks (GANs) have been applied in numerous fields, particularly in image synthesis, creative arts, and computer vision. Below are some key applications:

1. **Image Synthesis**:
   - GANs can generate realistic images from random noise, or even from partial or abstract inputs. This includes generating new images of people, objects, or scenes that resemble real data but are completely artificial.
   - **DeepFake** technology, where faces in videos or images are swapped, is one example of GAN-based image synthesis.

   Example: In fashion, GANs can generate realistic clothing designs based on existing trends, or in medical imaging, GANs can create synthetic MRI scans to augment training datasets.

2. **Style Transfer**:
   - **Style Transfer** is the process of taking the visual style of one image and applying it to another while preserving the content. GANs can be used

for this purpose to generate artistic versions of images, such as turning photographs into paintings or sketches.

o **CycleGANs** (a variation of GANs) have been particularly successful in style transfer applications, where they can transfer the style between domains (e.g., transforming photos into artwork or changing the season in landscape images).

Example: A photograph of a cityscape can be transformed into a painting that mimics the style of famous artists like Picasso or Van Gogh using GANs.

Real-World Example: Creating Art with GANs

One of the most creative applications of GANs is in **art generation**. GANs can be trained to produce entirely new pieces of art by learning from existing artworks or a specific style.

Steps for Creating Art with GANs:

1. **Dataset Collection**:
   o Collect a large dataset of artworks or images in the style you want to replicate. This could include classical art, abstract art, or modern digital art.
2. **Training the GAN**:

o Use a GAN to learn the features of the artwork style. For instance, if you're creating a GAN to generate paintings in the style of Van Gogh, the GAN would learn the brush strokes, color patterns, and textures characteristic of Van Gogh's work.

3. **Generating New Art**:

o Once the model is trained, it can generate new art by taking random noise as input and transforming it into images that resemble the learned style.

Example Code for Art Generation with GANs (using a pre-trained model):

python

```
import torch
from torchvision import models, transforms
from PIL import Image

# Load pre-trained GAN model (e.g., DCGAN or
StyleGAN)
model = torch.hub.load('pytorch/vision:v0.6.0',
'dcgan', pretrained=True)

# Load and preprocess the input image (e.g., a
photo)
image = Image.open("path_to_image.jpg")
```

208

```python
preprocess = transforms.Compose([
    transforms.Resize(256),
    transforms.CenterCrop(224),
    transforms.ToTensor(),
    transforms.Normalize(mean=[0.485,    0.456,
0.406], std=[0.229, 0.224, 0.225]),
])
input_tensor = preprocess(image)
input_batch = input_tensor.unsqueeze(0)    # Add
batch dimension

# Generate art using the trained model
with torch.no_grad():
    output = model(input_batch)

# Convert output to image and display
output_image = output.squeeze(0).permute(1, 2,
0).numpy()
output_image     =     (output_image     *
255).astype('uint8')
Image.fromarray(output_image).show()
```

In this example, we load a pre-trained GAN model and generate art based on an input image. While this code may require additional fine-tuning, it demonstrates the general process of using GANs for art generation.

Key Takeaways:

- **Generative Models** are machine learning models that generate new data points by learning the underlying distribution of the data.

- **Generative Adversarial Networks (GANs)** consist of two networks (generator and discriminator) that are trained adversarially to generate realistic data.

- **Applications of GANs** include **image synthesis** (generating realistic images) and **style transfer** (applying artistic styles to images).

- **Creating art with GANs** is an innovative use of this technology, allowing the generation of new artwork based on learned styles or input data.

In the next chapter, we will explore **Autoencoders**, another type of generative model used for tasks like dimensionality reduction, anomaly detection, and image reconstruction.

CHAPTER 21

TIME SERIES FORECASTING

Introduction to Time Series Analysis

Time series analysis is a technique used to analyze time-ordered data in order to extract meaningful statistics and other characteristics of the data. Time series data is a sequence of data points collected or recorded at successive points in time, typically at uniform intervals (e.g., daily, monthly, yearly). The goal of time series analysis is to understand the underlying patterns in the data, make forecasts, and identify potential trends, seasonalities, and cyclic behaviors.

Key components of time series data:

1. **Trend**: The long-term movement or direction in the data (e.g., increasing sales over several years).
2. **Seasonality**: Patterns that repeat at regular intervals, often within a year (e.g., increased retail sales during the holiday season).
3. **Cyclic Patterns**: Long-term fluctuations that do not have a fixed period (e.g., economic cycles).
4. **Noise**: Random fluctuations or irregularities in the data that cannot be explained by trends, seasonality, or cyclic patterns.

Time series forecasting is crucial in various fields such as economics, finance, sales, and healthcare. By identifying trends and seasonality, businesses can make data-driven decisions, such as adjusting inventory levels, optimizing staffing schedules, and planning marketing campaigns.

Methods for Time Series Forecasting: ARIMA, Exponential Smoothing

There are several traditional methods for time series forecasting, including **ARIMA** and **Exponential Smoothing**.

1. **ARIMA (AutoRegressive Integrated Moving Average)**: ARIMA is one of the most widely used methods for time series forecasting. It is based on three key components:
   - **AutoRegressive (AR)**: A model that uses the relationship between an observation and several lagged observations (previous time steps).
   - **Integrated (I)**: Differencing the data to make it stationary (i.e., removing trends and making the mean and variance constant over time).
   - **Moving Average (MA)**: A model that uses the relationship between an observation and the residual errors from a moving average model applied to lagged observations.

ARIMA Model Equation:

$Y_t = \mu + \phi_1 Y_{t-1} + \phi_2 Y_{t-2} + \dots + \phi_p Y_{t-p} + \theta_1 \epsilon_{t-1} + \theta_2 \epsilon_{t-2} + \dots + \theta_q \epsilon_{t-q} + \epsilon_t$

$Y_t = \mu + \phi_1 Y_{t-1} + \phi_2 Y_{t-2} + \dots + \phi_p Y_{t-p} + \theta_1 \epsilon_{t-1} + \theta_2 \epsilon_{t-2} + \dots + \theta_q \epsilon_{t-q} + \epsilon_t$

Where:

- Y_t is the value at time t,
- μ is the mean,
- ϕ and θ are the autoregressive and moving average parameters, respectively,
- ϵ_t is the error term.

Steps to Use ARIMA:

- **Stationarity**: Ensure the data is stationary by removing trends or seasonality.
- **Identify p, d, q**: Choose the appropriate values for the AR, I, and MA components using statistical tests like the ACF (Autocorrelation Function) and PACF (Partial Autocorrelation Function).
- **Fit the ARIMA Model**: Fit the model to the training data and make predictions.

213

Example in Python (ARIMA):

python

```
from statsmodels.tsa.arima.model import
ARIMA
from statsmodels.graphics.tsaplots import
plot_acf, plot_pacf

# Load time series data (example: monthly
sales data)
time_series_data                          =
pd.read_csv('sales_data.csv',
index_col='Date', parse_dates=True)

# Plot ACF and PACF to identify p and q
values
plot_acf(time_series_data)
plot_pacf(time_series_data)

# Fit the ARIMA model (example:
ARIMA(1,1,1))
model = ARIMA(time_series_data, order=(1,
1, 1))
model_fit = model.fit()

# Make predictions
forecast = model_fit.forecast(steps=12)  #
Predict the next 12 months
print(forecast)
```

214

2. **Exponential Smoothing**: Exponential Smoothing methods assign exponentially decreasing weights to past observations, making more recent observations more influential in the forecast. There are several variants:

    o   **Simple Exponential Smoothing**: Suitable for time series with no trend or seasonality.

    o   **Holt's Linear Trend Model**: Extends simple exponential smoothing to capture linear trends.

    o   **Holt-Winters Seasonal Model**: Adds seasonality to capture both trend and seasonal patterns.

Exponential Smoothing Formula:

    o   **Simple Exponential Smoothing**:

        y^t+1=αyt+(1−α)y^t\hat{y}_{t+1} = \alpha y_t + (1 - \alpha) \hat{y}_ty^t+1=αyt+(1−α)y^t

        Where   y^t+1\hat{y}_{t+1}y^t+1   is   the forecasted value for the next time step, α\alphaα is the smoothing factor, and yty_tyt is the actual value at time ttt.

Example in Python (Exponential Smoothing):

```python
```

215

```
from    statsmodels.tsa.holtwinters    import
ExponentialSmoothing

# Fit the Holt-Winters seasonal model
model                                          =
ExponentialSmoothing(time_series_data,
trend='add',                   seasonal='add',
seasonal_periods=12)
model_fit = model.fit()

# Forecast the next 12 periods
forecast = model_fit.forecast(steps=12)
print(forecast)
```

Using LSTMs for Time Series Prediction

While traditional methods like ARIMA and Exponential Smoothing are powerful, deep learning methods like **Long Short-Term Memory (LSTM)** networks have become increasingly popular for time series forecasting. LSTMs are a type of **Recurrent Neural Network (RNN)** that are particularly effective for sequence prediction tasks because they can capture long-term dependencies in the data.

Why Use LSTMs for Time Series?

- **Long-Term Dependencies**: LSTMs are able to remember information over long sequences, making them well-suited for time series data that exhibits long-term trends and seasonality.

- **Handling Complex Patterns**: LSTMs can learn complex relationships in time series data, such as non-linear trends, seasonality, and irregular fluctuations.

Steps for Using LSTMs in Time Series Forecasting:

1. **Data Preprocessing**: Normalize the data and reshape it into sequences of inputs and corresponding outputs.
2. **Build the LSTM Model**: Use LSTM layers to capture temporal dependencies.
3. **Train the Model**: Use the training data to adjust the model weights.
4. **Evaluate and Forecast**: Evaluate the model on the test set and use it to forecast future values.

Example Code for Time Series Prediction using LSTM:

```python
from tensorflow.keras.models import Sequential
from tensorflow.keras.layers import LSTM, Dense
from sklearn.preprocessing import MinMaxScaler
import numpy as np

# Load time series data (example: daily
temperature data)
```

217

```
data      =      pd.read_csv('temperature_data.csv',
index_col='Date', parse_dates=True)
data_values                                      =
data['Temperature'].values.reshape(-1, 1)

# Normalize the data
scaler = MinMaxScaler(feature_range=(0, 1))
scaled_data = scaler.fit_transform(data_values)

# Prepare the data for LSTM (sequence of 60 time
steps)
def create_dataset(data, time_step=60):
    X, y = [], []
    for i in range(len(data) - time_step - 1):
        X.append(data[i:(i + time_step), 0])
        y.append(data[i + time_step, 0])
    return np.array(X), np.array(y)

X, y = create_dataset(scaled_data)
X = X.reshape(X.shape[0], X.shape[1], 1)    #
Reshape for LSTM (samples, time steps, features)

# Build the LSTM model
model = Sequential()
model.add(LSTM(units=50, return_sequences=False,
input_shape=(X.shape[1], 1)))
model.add(Dense(units=1))

# Compile and train the model
```

```
model.compile(optimizer='adam',
loss='mean_squared_error')
model.fit(X, y, epochs=10, batch_size=32)

# Make predictions
predictions = model.predict(X)
predictions                                    =
scaler.inverse_transform(predictions)
print(predictions)
```

In this example, we build an LSTM model to predict future temperature values based on historical data. The LSTM learns the temporal dependencies and can make accurate forecasts for future time steps.

Real-World Example: Sales Prediction for a Retail Store

Sales prediction is a critical task in retail, as it helps businesses optimize inventory management, staffing, and marketing strategies. Time series forecasting can be used to predict future sales based on historical data.

1. **Data Collection**: Gather historical sales data, including daily or weekly sales figures, promotional activities, holidays, and other factors that might affect sales.

2. **Data Preprocessing**: Clean and preprocess the data by removing outliers, handling missing values, and normalizing the data.

3. **Model Training**: Use traditional methods like ARIMA or modern deep learning methods like LSTMs to build a model that can predict future sales.

4. **Model Evaluation**: Evaluate the model on a validation set and test its ability to generalize to unseen data.

5. **Forecasting**: Use the trained model to forecast future sales, helping the business plan for demand fluctuations and optimize stock levels.

Key Takeaways:

- **Time Series Analysis** involves understanding and forecasting sequential data with components like trends, seasonality, and noise.

- **ARIMA** and **Exponential Smoothing** are traditional statistical methods for time series forecasting.

- **LSTMs** are deep learning models that are well-suited for capturing long-term dependencies in time series data, and are increasingly used for tasks like sales prediction.

- **Real-World Example**: Time series forecasting can be applied to predict future sales for a retail store, helping businesses optimize inventory and improve decision-making.

In the next chapter, we will explore **Reinforcement Learning for Real-Time Decision Making**, where we will dive deeper into how reinforcement learning is used for decision-making in dynamic, real-time environments.

CHAPTER 22

ANOMALY DETECTION AND OUTLIER DETECTION

What is Anomaly Detection?

Anomaly detection, also known as outlier detection, refers to the process of identifying data points that deviate significantly from the normal behavior of a system or dataset. These data points, called **anomalies** or **outliers**, can indicate critical incidents, such as fraud, network intrusions, or defects in manufacturing processes.

Anomalies can occur in various forms:

- **Point anomalies**: Single data points that are far removed from the rest of the data (e.g., an unusually large bank withdrawal).
- **Contextual anomalies**: Data points that are anomalous within a specific context but not necessarily outside that context (e.g., a spike in sales during the holiday season).
- **Collective anomalies**: A group of data points that are collectively anomalous, though individual points may not seem so (e.g., a sudden surge in failed login attempts).

Anomaly detection is crucial in areas such as fraud detection, network security, fault detection in systems, and healthcare for identifying outliers that may indicate a medical condition.

Techniques for Anomaly Detection: Isolation Forest, DBSCAN

There are several methods available for anomaly detection, ranging from statistical techniques to machine learning algorithms. We will cover two popular methods: **Isolation Forest** and **DBSCAN**.

1. **Isolation Forest**:
    o **Isolation Forest** is an ensemble-based anomaly detection algorithm that works by isolating anomalies instead of profiling normal data points. It isolates points that are fewer in number (anomalies) by recursively partitioning the data.
    o The main idea is that anomalies are easier to isolate because they differ from the majority of the data points. Isolation Forest uses a decision tree approach to partition the data into smaller regions, and the anomalies are identified by how easily they are separated from the rest of the data.

Key advantages:

    o Efficient: Works well on high-dimensional datasets.

223

- o Scalable: Performs efficiently even on large datasets with a large number of features.

Example Code for Isolation Forest:

python

```
from        sklearn.ensemble        import
IsolationForest
import numpy as np

# Generate some data with anomalies
data = np.random.randn(100, 2)
anomalies   =   np.random.uniform(low=-5,
high=5, size=(5, 2))   # Add some anomalies
data_with_anomalies   =   np.vstack([data,
anomalies])

# Initialize the Isolation Forest model
model                                   =
IsolationForest(contamination=0.05)   # Set
contamination to the expected proportion of
anomalies

# Fit the model to the data
model.fit(data_with_anomalies)

# Predict anomalies (1 for normal points,
-1 for anomalies)
```

```
predictions                                    =
model.predict(data_with_anomalies)

print("Predictions:", predictions)
```

In this example, we generate synthetic data and use Isolation Forest to detect anomalies. The `contamination` parameter indicates the expected proportion of anomalies in the dataset, and the model assigns a label of 1 (normal) or -1 (anomaly) to each data point.

2. **DBSCAN (Density-Based Spatial Clustering of Applications with Noise)**:
   - o **DBSCAN** is a density-based clustering algorithm that can also be used for anomaly detection. It identifies regions of high point density and considers points in low-density regions as anomalies (outliers).
   - o DBSCAN is particularly effective for detecting **contextual anomalies** where the data points form clusters, but some points lie outside the clusters and are considered anomalies.
   - o DBSCAN requires two parameters:
     - **Epsilon (ε\epsilonϵ)**: Defines the maximum distance between two points to be considered neighbors.

225

- **MinPts**: The minimum number of points required to form a dense region (i.e., a cluster).

Key advantages:

- o Can detect anomalies of arbitrary shapes.
- o Does not require the number of clusters to be specified.
- o Can handle noise effectively.

Example Code for DBSCAN:

```python
from sklearn.cluster import DBSCAN
import numpy as np

# Generate some data with anomalies
data = np.random.randn(100, 2)
anomalies = np.random.uniform(low=-5,
high=5, size=(5, 2))  # Add some anomalies
data_with_anomalies = np.vstack([data,
anomalies])

# Initialize the DBSCAN model
model = DBSCAN(eps=0.5, min_samples=5)

# Fit the model to the data
```

226

```
labels                              =
model.fit_predict(data_with_anomalies)

print("Labels:", labels)   # -1 indicates
anomalies
```

In this example, DBSCAN detects anomalies by labeling points that do not belong to any cluster with the label -1.

Real-World Example: Fraud Detection in Credit Card Transactions

Anomaly detection plays a crucial role in **fraud detection**, particularly in areas like **credit card transactions**, where fraudulent activities (such as unauthorized purchases) can be detected by identifying unusual patterns in transaction data.

1. **Problem Overview**:
   - In a typical scenario, a credit card company needs to detect anomalous transactions that might indicate fraudulent activity.
   - Fraudulent transactions usually differ significantly from regular transactions in terms of amount, location, time, and frequency.
2. **Approach**:
   - We can use anomaly detection techniques to analyze transaction data, such as the amount, merchant, and geographical location.

227

o If a transaction deviates from the normal behavior of the user, it is flagged as an anomaly for further investigation.

3. **Data**:

o The dataset may contain features like:

- **Amount**: The amount of the transaction.
- **Merchant**: The merchant or location where the transaction occurred.
- **Time**: The time of the transaction.
- **User ID**: The ID of the cardholder.

4. **Modeling**: Using **Isolation Forest** or **DBSCAN**, we can train an anomaly detection model on historical transaction data. Transactions that deviate significantly from the normal patterns will be flagged as potential fraud.

Example Code for Fraud Detection using Isolation Forest:

python

```
from        sklearn.ensemble         import
IsolationForest
import pandas as pd

# Load the transaction data (for example,
'transactions.csv'   containing   features
like 'amount', 'user_id')
data = pd.read_csv('transactions.csv')
```

```python
# Preprocess the data (e.g., normalization,
handling categorical data)
# Assuming 'amount' is the primary feature
we want to analyze for anomalies
amount_data                             =
data['amount'].values.reshape(-1, 1)

# Train the Isolation Forest model
model                                   =
IsolationForest(contamination=0.05)  # Set
the  expected  anomaly  rate  (5%  of
transactions)
model.fit(amount_data)

# Predict anomalies
predictions = model.predict(amount_data)

# Anomalies are labeled as -1
data['is_anomaly'] = predictions
fraud_transactions                      =
data[data['is_anomaly'] == -1]
print(fraud_transactions)
```

In this example, the model is trained on the `amount` feature of transaction data and used to detect anomalous transactions. The `contamination` parameter is set to 5%, indicating that we expect 5% of the transactions to be fraudulent.

5. **Model Evaluation**:

- o To evaluate the model, we can use labeled data (if available) to compare the detected anomalies with known fraudulent transactions.

- o Common evaluation metrics for anomaly detection include **precision**, **recall**, **F1-score**, and **area under the ROC curve (AUC)**.

Key Takeaways:

- **Anomaly Detection** is the process of identifying unusual data points that deviate significantly from normal patterns.

- **Isolation Forest** is an efficient anomaly detection method that isolates anomalies by creating decision trees.

- **DBSCAN** is a density-based method that can detect anomalies in datasets with complex structures and varying densities.

- **Real-World Example**: Fraud detection in credit card transactions can be accomplished by identifying anomalous transaction behaviors using models like Isolation Forest.

In the next chapter, we will explore **Model Interpretability and Explainability**, focusing on techniques and tools to understand

and explain how machine learning models make their predictions, ensuring trust and transparency in AI systems.

CHAPTER 23

ETHICAL CONSIDERATIONS IN MACHINE LEARNING

Bias in Machine Learning Models

Bias in machine learning models refers to systematic errors that occur when the model's predictions are influenced by prejudiced assumptions, historical inequalities, or skewed data. Bias in AI systems can lead to unfair outcomes, perpetuating discrimination and reinforcing stereotypes. Bias can be introduced at various stages of the machine learning pipeline, including data collection, feature selection, and model training.

1. **Types of Bias**:
    - **Data Bias**: Occurs when the training data does not adequately represent the real-world population, leading the model to favor certain groups over others. For example, if a facial recognition system is trained primarily on light-skinned individuals, it may have lower accuracy for dark-skinned individuals.
    - **Label Bias**: Happens when labels in the training data are inaccurately assigned due to human error, cultural bias, or other subjective factors.

- o **Sampling Bias**: Arises when the data sample is not representative of the population, such as when certain demographic groups are underrepresented.

- o **Measurement Bias**: Occurs when data is inaccurately measured or recorded, which can distort the model's predictions.

2. **Examples of Bias**:

    - o **Hiring Algorithms**: If a machine learning model used for recruitment is trained on historical hiring data where certain groups (e.g., women or minorities) were underrepresented, the model may favor candidates from overrepresented groups.

    - o **Criminal Justice**: Predictive models used in sentencing or parole decisions may exhibit bias if they are trained on biased data (e.g., historical data that reflects racial disparities in policing or sentencing).

3. **Addressing Bias**:

    - o **Balanced Data**: Ensuring that the training data represents all groups equally can help reduce bias.

    - o **Bias Audits**: Regularly auditing models for fairness and bias can help detect issues early and ensure that the model is not discriminating against certain groups.

- o **Fairness Metrics**: Use fairness metrics, such as **demographic parity** (equal representation across groups) or **equal opportunity** (ensuring equal true positive rates across groups), to evaluate and mitigate bias in models.

The Impact of Unbiased Data and Fairness

Ensuring that machine learning models are trained on unbiased data is crucial for achieving **fairness**. Fairness refers to the concept that AI systems should treat all individuals or groups impartially and equitably. When models are fair, they do not disproportionately disadvantage any particular group based on protected characteristics like race, gender, or socioeconomic status.

1. **Why Fairness Matters**:
   - o **Social Justice**: Unfair or biased models can perpetuate inequality, negatively impacting vulnerable groups and exacerbating societal disparities.
   - o **Trust**: Models that are seen as biased or unfair can erode trust in AI systems, especially in sensitive areas like criminal justice, hiring, and healthcare.

o **Legal and Regulatory Compliance**: Many countries have laws that require non-discriminatory practices in areas like hiring, lending, and healthcare. Ensuring fairness in machine learning models is necessary for compliance with these regulations.

2. **Approaches to Ensuring Fairness**:

   o **Fair Representation**: Ensure that training data reflects a diverse set of individuals and scenarios, so that the model learns unbiased patterns.

   o **Bias Mitigation Algorithms**: Algorithms such as **adversarial debiasing** or **fair representations learning** can be used to modify the training process in order to reduce bias and increase fairness.

   o **Post-Hoc Fairness Analysis**: After a model is trained, post-hoc fairness checks can be performed to detect and correct any biases that have emerged in the model's predictions.

3. **Examples of Fairness in Practice**:

   o **Equal Opportunity in Healthcare**: Ensuring that AI systems used in medical diagnoses do not favor certain demographics over others, which could lead to unequal access to healthcare.

   o **Fair Lending Models**: Credit scoring models should be designed to avoid discrimination

235

against certain racial, ethnic, or gender groups in lending decisions.

Transparency in AI Models: Explainable AI (XAI)

Explainable AI (XAI) refers to the development of machine learning models that provide human-readable explanations for their predictions and decisions. While deep learning models, such as neural networks, often operate as "black boxes" that are difficult to interpret, XAI aims to make these models more transparent, interpretable, and trustworthy.

1. **Why Transparency Matters**:
    - **Accountability**: Transparent models allow developers and users to understand why a certain decision was made, making it easier to hold systems accountable for their actions.
    - **Trust**: Users are more likely to trust AI systems that can explain their decisions, especially in critical areas like healthcare, finance, and criminal justice.
    - **Regulation**: Some industries require transparency in decision-making, particularly when it affects individuals' rights or well-being.
2. **Techniques for Explainability**:

236

- o **LIME (Local Interpretable Model-agnostic Explanations)**: LIME explains the predictions of any machine learning classifier by approximating it with an interpretable model (such as linear regression) locally around a prediction.
- o **SHAP (SHapley Additive exPlanations)**: SHAP values provide a unified measure of feature importance for machine learning models, based on game theory principles. SHAP explains the contribution of each feature to a particular prediction.
- o **Feature Importance**: For simpler models like decision trees or linear regression, feature importance can directly tell you which features contributed most to the model's predictions.
- o **Saliency Maps**: For deep learning models (e.g., convolutional neural networks), saliency maps highlight which parts of an image contributed most to the prediction, helping interpret the model's decisions.

3. **Challenges in XAI**:
   - o **Trade-Off with Performance**: Sometimes, more explainable models (like decision trees) may be less powerful than complex models (like deep neural networks). Balancing interpretability and performance is an ongoing challenge.

237

o **Complexity**: Even with explainability techniques, highly complex models may still be difficult for humans to interpret fully, leading to a need for continual improvement in explanation methods.

Ethical Challenges in Automated Decision Making

Automated decision-making systems powered by AI and machine learning are increasingly being used to make decisions in sensitive areas such as hiring, healthcare, credit scoring, criminal justice, and loan approvals. While these systems have the potential to streamline processes and improve efficiency, they also raise significant ethical concerns.

1. **Bias in Decision Making**:
   o As discussed earlier, bias in training data can result in unfair or discriminatory decisions. This can particularly impact marginalized groups in areas such as hiring or criminal justice. If the historical data used to train the model reflects systemic bias, the model may perpetuate those biases in its decisions.

2. **Lack of Human Oversight**:
   o Fully automating decision-making processes can remove human oversight, making it difficult to

238

intervene or challenge the outcomes. In areas like healthcare or criminal justice, human judgment is essential to ensuring ethical decisions are made, particularly in complex or ambiguous cases.

3. **Privacy Concerns**:
   o AI systems often require large amounts of personal data to make accurate predictions. This raises privacy concerns, especially when sensitive information (such as medical history or financial data) is used to make decisions. Ethical considerations must ensure that data is handled securely and that individuals' privacy rights are respected.

4. **Accountability and Responsibility**:
   o If an AI system makes an incorrect or harmful decision (such as denying a loan or recommending incorrect medical treatment), it is not always clear who is responsible: the developer, the company deploying the system, or the model itself? Ensuring clear accountability for AI-driven decisions is essential to avoid situations where harm is done without recourse.

5. **Transparency and Explainability**:
   o In automated decision-making, it is essential for AI models to be **transparent** and **explainable** to ensure that stakeholders understand how

decisions are made and can challenge them if necessary. Lack of transparency can erode trust in the system, especially in high-stakes scenarios like healthcare and law enforcement.

Key Takeaways:

- **Bias in Machine Learning Models**: Bias in data and models can lead to unfair, discriminatory, and unethical outcomes. Mitigating bias is crucial for ensuring fairness in AI systems.

- **Fairness and Unbiased Data**: Fairness in machine learning models ensures that all groups are treated equally, and models are designed to avoid discriminatory behavior.

- **Transparency and Explainability**: Explainable AI (XAI) aims to make machine learning models more interpretable, improving trust and accountability.

- **Ethical Challenges in Automated Decision Making**: Ethical concerns such as bias, lack of human oversight, privacy, and accountability need to be addressed when deploying AI systems in decision-making processes.

In the next chapter, we will explore **AI Governance and Regulations**, focusing on the legal, ethical, and societal frameworks that guide the responsible development and deployment of AI systems.

CHAPTER 24

MACHINE LEARNING IN THE REAL WORLD: INDUSTRY APPLICATIONS

Machine Learning in Healthcare: Predicting Diseases

Machine learning has tremendous potential in the healthcare industry, where it can be used to improve diagnostics, predict diseases, and personalize treatment plans. ML algorithms can process vast amounts of medical data, including patient records, medical images, and genomic data, to identify patterns that may not be immediately apparent to human doctors.

Key Applications in Healthcare:

1. **Disease Prediction**: Machine learning models are increasingly being used to predict the likelihood of diseases based on patient data. For example, ML algorithms can analyze patient history, lifestyle factors, genetic information, and clinical test results to predict the onset of chronic diseases like diabetes, heart disease, and cancer.

Example: A deep learning model can be trained on patient data (age, weight, smoking status, blood pressure) to predict the likelihood of developing heart disease in the future. Early identification allows for timely interventions and preventive measures.

2. **Medical Imaging**: Machine learning, especially **convolutional neural networks (CNNs)**, is widely used in medical imaging to detect anomalies such as tumors in CT scans, MRIs, or X-rays. These models can assist radiologists in detecting diseases like cancer, pneumonia, or neurological disorders with high accuracy.

    Example: A CNN can be trained to detect lung cancer by analyzing medical images, reducing the workload of radiologists and providing faster diagnosis.

3. **Personalized Medicine**: By analyzing patient data, machine learning can also aid in **personalized medicine**, where treatment plans are tailored based on the individual's specific genetic makeup, lifestyle, and response to previous treatments. ML models can predict how a patient will respond to certain medications, thus helping in choosing the most effective drugs.

Machine Learning in Finance: Risk Analysis, Fraud Detection

The finance industry uses machine learning extensively for risk analysis, fraud detection, and algorithmic trading. By analyzing historical data and market conditions, ML algorithms can provide more accurate forecasts, detect suspicious activities, and optimize financial decision-making processes.

1. **Risk Analysis**: In finance, **risk analysis** refers to the process of assessing the potential risks involved in investments or lending. Machine learning models are used to analyze historical market data, economic indicators, and individual financial profiles to predict the risk associated with a specific investment or loan.

   Example: A bank may use ML models to evaluate the creditworthiness of loan applicants. The model can analyze factors like credit scores, income, past debts, and other financial metrics to determine the risk of default and set appropriate interest rates.

2. **Fraud Detection**: Fraud detection is a critical application of machine learning in finance. By analyzing transaction data, ML algorithms can identify unusual or suspicious patterns that may indicate fraudulent activity, such as identity theft or money laundering.

244

Example: Credit card companies use machine learning to analyze transaction patterns and detect fraudulent charges in real-time. If a customer typically makes small purchases in one location and a large transaction occurs in a distant country, the system can flag it for further investigation.

3. **Algorithmic Trading**: Machine learning models can be used in **algorithmic trading**, where algorithms make stock market decisions at high speeds. These models can analyze massive amounts of market data and make decisions in real-time based on patterns or predictions about stock movements.

   Example: Hedge funds and trading firms use ML models to predict stock prices and execute trades automatically. These systems can identify trends, correlations, and patterns that might be missed by human traders.

Machine Learning in Retail: Personalized Recommendations

Machine learning is widely used in the retail industry to enhance customer experience, optimize inventory management, and improve marketing strategies. **Personalized recommendation systems** are one of the most popular applications of ML in retail, where algorithms suggest products to customers based on their preferences and behavior.

1. **Personalized Recommendations**: Recommendation systems are used by online retailers like Amazon, Netflix, and Spotify to suggest products, movies, or music to users. These systems analyze user behavior, including previous purchases, browsing history, and interactions with the platform, to recommend items that a user is likely to purchase or enjoy.

   Example: Amazon uses collaborative filtering to recommend products to users based on the preferences of similar customers. If a user frequently purchases tech gadgets, the system will suggest related items such as accessories or complementary products.

2. **Customer Segmentation**: Machine learning can also be used to segment customers based on their purchasing habits, demographics, or interactions with the brand. This segmentation enables retailers to target specific groups of customers with personalized marketing campaigns and promotions.

   Example: A clothing retailer may use clustering algorithms to segment customers into groups such as "frequent buyers," "price-sensitive shoppers," and "brand loyalists," allowing for tailored advertising and sales strategies for each segment.

3. **Demand Forecasting and Inventory Optimization**: ML models can forecast demand for products based on factors such as seasonality, trends, historical sales data, and external factors like holidays or weather. By accurately predicting demand, retailers can optimize inventory levels, reducing overstocking or stockouts.

   Example: A supermarket chain may use time series forecasting models to predict the demand for products like fresh produce or seasonal items, ensuring they stock the right quantities at the right time.

Real-World Case Studies from Different Industries

Machine learning is transforming various industries by automating processes, improving decision-making, and creating new opportunities for growth. Below are some real-world case studies showcasing the power of ML in diverse industries:

1. **Healthcare: Predicting Disease Outbreaks**: The **World Health Organization (WHO)** uses machine learning to predict the outbreak of diseases like Ebola, Zika, and COVID-19. By analyzing various data sources, including historical health data, weather patterns, and travel data,

ML models can predict outbreaks and help allocate resources more effectively.

Example: During the COVID-19 pandemic, machine learning models were used to predict the spread of the virus, helping governments and health organizations implement timely interventions and policies.

2. **Finance: Credit Scoring and Loan Approval**: **FICO**, a global analytics company, uses machine learning algorithms to assess creditworthiness and provide credit scores. By analyzing transaction histories, repayment patterns, and other financial metrics, the system can provide more accurate and inclusive credit scoring, reducing the likelihood of defaults.

   Example: **LendingClub**, a peer-to-peer lending company, uses machine learning to predict the likelihood of loan defaults and determine appropriate interest rates for borrowers.

3. **Retail: Customer Behavior Prediction**: **Walmart** uses machine learning to optimize its supply chain by predicting customer purchasing behavior. By analyzing historical sales data, seasonality, and promotions, Walmart can predict which products will be in demand and ensure that they are stocked at the right locations.

Example: **Netflix** uses machine learning to recommend movies and TV shows based on individual user preferences. Their system uses collaborative filtering, matrix factorization, and deep learning to suggest content that users are most likely to enjoy.

4. **Transportation: Autonomous Vehicles**: **Tesla** uses machine learning to train its self-driving cars. By processing large amounts of sensor data (camera images, radar, lidar, etc.), Tesla's ML models allow its vehicles to understand and navigate their environment, detecting obstacles, recognizing traffic signs, and making driving decisions in real-time.

Example: **Waymo**, a subsidiary of Alphabet (Google), uses machine learning to power its autonomous vehicles, enabling them to drive safely and efficiently in urban environments.

Key Takeaways:

- **Machine Learning in Healthcare**: ML can predict diseases, assist in diagnostics, and personalize treatment plans, improving patient care and outcomes.

- **Machine Learning in Finance**: ML is used for risk analysis, fraud detection, and algorithmic trading, optimizing financial decision-making.
- **Machine Learning in Retail**: Retailers use ML for personalized recommendations, customer segmentation, and demand forecasting, improving customer satisfaction and operational efficiency.
- **Real-World Case Studies**: ML is transforming industries like healthcare, finance, retail, and transportation by automating processes, improving decision-making, and creating new opportunities.

In the next chapter, we will explore **The Future of Machine Learning**, focusing on emerging trends, challenges, and opportunities in AI and ML that will shape the future of industries and society.

CHAPTER 25

CHALLENGES AND LIMITATIONS OF MACHINE LEARNING

Data Quality and Availability

Data is the foundation of machine learning, and its quality directly affects the performance and accuracy of models. Inadequate, poor-quality, or insufficient data can lead to unreliable models and inaccurate predictions. Some of the common data-related challenges faced in machine learning are:

1. **Data Quality**:
   o **Missing Data**: Missing or incomplete data can cause biases and inaccuracies in model predictions. Machine learning algorithms rely on complete and clean data to learn effectively. Imputation techniques or simply removing missing data points are common solutions.
   o **Noisy Data**: Noisy data contains random errors or fluctuations that can mislead models. Noise can come from sensor errors, incorrect labels, or human mistakes in data collection. Techniques like data smoothing, outlier detection, and robust modeling approaches can help handle noise.

- ○ **Incorrect Labels**: In supervised learning, inaccurate labeling of data can severely affect model performance, leading to erroneous predictions. Ensuring accurate labeling through quality control and manual verification is essential.

2. **Data Availability**:

   - ○ **Limited Data**: Machine learning models, especially deep learning models, require large amounts of data to generalize well. When data is scarce, models may overfit, meaning they perform well on the training set but fail to generalize to new, unseen data.

   - ○ **Data Privacy**: In fields like healthcare or finance, data may be restricted due to privacy concerns or regulations (e.g., HIPAA in the U.S., GDPR in Europe). Collecting and using such data in a responsible manner while maintaining privacy can be challenging.

   - ○ **Imbalanced Data**: In some cases, the classes in the dataset may be imbalanced (e.g., fraud detection datasets with far fewer fraudulent transactions than non-fraudulent ones). Imbalanced datasets can cause models to bias predictions towards the majority class. Techniques like **oversampling**, **undersampling**, and using different evaluation metrics (e.g., precision, recall) can help address this issue.

3. **Solution Strategies**:

   o **Data Augmentation**: When data is limited, especially in domains like image and text data, data augmentation techniques can be used to artificially expand the dataset.

   o **Synthetic Data Generation**: In certain cases, synthetic data generated by methods like **GANs (Generative Adversarial Networks)** can be used to supplement real-world data.

Overfitting and Underfitting

Two of the most common challenges in machine learning are **overfitting** and **underfitting**. Both refer to how well a model generalizes to new, unseen data, and they are critical to achieving a balance between bias and variance.

1. **Overfitting**:

   o **Overfitting** occurs when a machine learning model learns the details and noise in the training data to the extent that it negatively impacts the model's performance on new data. Essentially, the model becomes too complex and captures

253

patterns that don't generalize to the broader population.

- ○ **Symptoms of Overfitting**:
  - ▪ High accuracy on the training data but poor performance on the validation or test data.
  - ▪ The model learns trivial patterns, such as small fluctuations or noise, that are specific to the training data.

Solutions to Overfitting:

- ○ **Cross-Validation**: Using cross-validation techniques (e.g., k-fold cross-validation) helps assess the model's performance across different subsets of the training data, which can prevent overfitting.
- ○ **Regularization**: Regularization methods such as **L1 (Lasso)** and **L2 (Ridge)** penalize large coefficients or complex models, thereby helping to prevent overfitting by keeping the model simpler.
- ○ **Early Stopping**: In iterative training methods (e.g., deep learning), stopping the training process when performance on a validation set starts to degrade can prevent the model from overfitting.

- o **Pruning**: In decision tree-based models, pruning is a technique that involves cutting back branches that add little predictive value, thus reducing the model complexity.

2. **Underfitting**:

   - o **Underfitting** occurs when a machine learning model is too simple to capture the underlying patterns in the data. This typically happens when the model lacks the necessary complexity, which results in poor performance on both the training and testing datasets.

   - o **Symptoms of Underfitting**:
     - Low accuracy on both the training and test datasets.
     - The model is too simplistic to capture key relationships in the data, such as using a linear model to capture a non-linear relationship.

   Solutions to Underfitting:

   - o **Increasing Model Complexity**: Use more complex models or add more features that better represent the data. For example, in linear regression, adding interaction terms between features may help capture non-linear relationships.

- o **Feature Engineering**: Carefully selecting or constructing features that help represent the data more meaningfully can improve model performance.
- o **Improving Data Quality**: Better quality data with more relevant features can help a model perform better.

The Curse of Dimensionality

The **curse of dimensionality** refers to the challenges that arise when working with high-dimensional data. As the number of features (dimensions) increases, the amount of data required to adequately train the model grows exponentially. This leads to several issues:

1. **Data Sparsity**:
   - o In high-dimensional spaces, the data becomes sparse, meaning there are fewer data points per unit of volume. This sparsity can cause the model to struggle in generalizing and identifying useful patterns.

2. **Increased Computation**:
   - o The computational complexity of training machine learning models increases significantly as the number of features increases. For instance,

in k-nearest neighbors (KNN), the distance between data points becomes less meaningful in high-dimensional spaces, leading to slower computations and inefficient models.

3. **Overfitting**:
   o High-dimensional datasets tend to have more opportunities for the model to find spurious correlations, which can lead to overfitting. The model may learn the noise in the data instead of true underlying patterns.

4. **Solution Strategies**:
   o **Dimensionality Reduction**: Techniques like **Principal Component Analysis (PCA)** and **t-SNE** can be used to reduce the number of dimensions while preserving the important characteristics of the data.
   o **Feature Selection**: By selecting a subset of relevant features, you can reduce the dimensionality without losing important information.
   o **Regularization**: Techniques like **L1 regularization (Lasso)** and **L2 regularization (Ridge)** can be used to constrain the complexity of the model and reduce the impact of irrelevant or redundant features.

257

Limitations of Deep Learning Models

While deep learning models, such as convolutional neural networks (CNNs) and recurrent neural networks (RNNs), have achieved remarkable success in various domains like image processing, natural language processing, and speech recognition, they also come with several limitations.

1. **Data Requirements**:
   o Deep learning models require vast amounts of labeled data to achieve optimal performance. In domains where labeled data is scarce or expensive to obtain, deep learning may not be the best choice.

   Example: In medical imaging, manually labeling large datasets of X-rays or MRI scans can be time-consuming and costly.

2. **Computational Resources**:
   o Deep learning models are computationally expensive and require powerful hardware, such as GPUs or TPUs, to train efficiently. This can make deep learning models inaccessible for smaller organizations or individuals with limited resources.

3. **Interpretability**:

o Deep learning models are often considered **black boxes**, meaning their decision-making process is not easily interpretable. This lack of transparency can be problematic in high-stakes applications such as healthcare, finance, and law enforcement, where understanding how a model makes decisions is crucial for trust and accountability.

Solution: **Explainable AI (XAI)** techniques like LIME or SHAP can be used to improve model interpretability and increase trust in the results.

4. **Overfitting and Generalization**:

o Deep learning models, especially those with many parameters, are prone to overfitting, particularly when training data is limited. Regularization techniques, such as **dropout** or **early stopping**, are needed to prevent overfitting.

5. **Training Time**:

o Training deep learning models can be time-consuming, especially for large datasets. This long training time can hinder experimentation and model iteration, especially in rapidly changing fields like e-commerce or real-time data applications.

259

Key Takeaways:

- **Data Quality and Availability**: The quality and availability of data are crucial for building reliable machine learning models. Bias, missing data, and imbalanced datasets can significantly impact model performance.

- **Overfitting and Underfitting**: Overfitting and underfitting are common problems that occur when a model is either too complex or too simple for the data. Balancing complexity is key to achieving good generalization.

- **The Curse of Dimensionality**: High-dimensional data can cause sparsity, overfitting, and increased computation. Dimensionality reduction techniques and feature selection are often necessary for handling large datasets.

- **Limitations of Deep Learning**: Deep learning models require large amounts of data, computational resources, and can suffer from interpretability issues. Despite their successes, these limitations make them unsuitable for every task.

In the next chapter, we will explore **The Future of Machine Learning**, focusing on emerging trends, innovations, and challenges in the AI field that will shape the future of technology.

CHAPTER 26

THE FUTURE OF MACHINE LEARNING AND AI

Emerging Trends: Federated Learning, Quantum Computing, AI Ethics

Machine learning and artificial intelligence are evolving rapidly, and several emerging trends are shaping the future of these technologies. These innovations promise to revolutionize industries, address new challenges, and provide more powerful tools for solving complex problems.

1. **Federated Learning**:
   - **Federated learning** is a decentralized approach to machine learning where the model is trained across multiple devices or servers that hold local data, without the data ever leaving those devices. Instead of sending data to a central server, the model learns locally on the device and shares only updates to the model parameters.
   - **Benefits**:
     - **Data Privacy**: Since the raw data never leaves the device, federated learning

261

helps preserve privacy and meet regulatory requirements (e.g., GDPR).

- **Reduced Latency**: By processing data locally, federated learning can reduce the time it takes to train a model, particularly in edge devices such as smartphones and IoT devices.
- **Scalability**: Federated learning allows models to be trained on a vast number of devices, harnessing the computational power of many devices without needing large-scale centralized infrastructure.

Example: Google's **Gboard** keyboard uses federated learning to improve its language models by learning from users' typing behavior directly on their devices, without sending sensitive data to servers.

2. **Quantum Computing**:
   - **Quantum computing** is a cutting-edge field that leverages the principles of quantum mechanics to perform calculations that are intractable for classical computers. Quantum computing has the potential to exponentially increase computational power and speed, particularly for complex tasks like optimization, cryptography, and machine learning.

- o **Impact on Machine Learning**:
  - • **Quantum Machine Learning (QML)** is an emerging area where quantum computers are used to improve traditional machine learning algorithms, particularly in areas like **data classification**, **pattern recognition**, and **clustering**. Quantum computers can process large datasets with immense speed, potentially transforming industries like finance, healthcare, and material science.
  - • **Quantum Superposition and Entanglement** can allow models to explore a wider set of possibilities faster than classical approaches.

Example: **Google** and **IBM** are leading the way in developing quantum computing platforms that could one day be used to speed up training processes for machine learning models and handle much larger datasets.

3. **AI Ethics**:
   - o As AI and machine learning systems become more integral to everyday life, ethical concerns are increasingly at the forefront. AI ethics focuses on the responsible development and deployment

263

of AI technologies to ensure they are used fairly, transparently, and for the benefit of all.

- ○ **Key Ethical Issues**:
  - ▪ **Bias and Fairness**: Ensuring that AI systems are free from bias and do not discriminate against specific groups based on gender, race, or other factors.
  - ▪ **Transparency and Explainability**: As AI models become more complex, ensuring that these systems are understandable and interpretable is critical for building trust and accountability.
  - ▪ **Privacy**: Protecting personal data and ensuring that AI systems respect privacy rights is a fundamental ethical concern.
  - ▪ **Accountability**: Determining who is responsible when AI systems make harmful decisions, especially in critical applications like healthcare, criminal justice, and autonomous vehicles.

Example: The **Ethics Guidelines for Trustworthy AI** by the European Commission outlines principles such as transparency, accountability, and fairness, aimed at ensuring AI technologies are developed and used ethically.

Automation and AI's Impact on Jobs

The widespread adoption of AI and machine learning is poised to transform the job market. While AI will automate many tasks, it will also create new opportunities and demand for new skills. The impact of AI on jobs can be understood in two primary ways:

1. **Job Displacement**:
   - **Automation of Routine Tasks**: AI and automation technologies are particularly effective at replacing repetitive and routine tasks that were previously performed by humans. This includes tasks such as data entry, scheduling, basic customer service, and even driving (in the case of autonomous vehicles).
   - **Industries Affected**: Manufacturing, logistics, retail, and administrative support are likely to see significant job displacement as AI systems take over tasks traditionally done by workers. For example, **self-checkout systems** and **robots** in warehouses are already replacing jobs in retail and logistics.

2. **Job Creation**:
   - **New Roles and Opportunities**: As AI and machine learning become more widespread, new roles and career opportunities will emerge. These include jobs in AI development, data science, AI

ethics, and human-AI collaboration. Roles such as **AI trainer**, **data scientist**, **robotics technician**, and **AI ethicist** are becoming increasingly important.

- ○ **Job Transformation**: Many existing jobs will evolve rather than disappear. For example, customer service agents may shift to roles that involve managing AI-powered chatbots or solving more complex issues that require human judgment. Healthcare professionals may use AI tools to enhance diagnosis and treatment but will remain essential for patient care and decision-making.

- ○ **Reskilling and Upskilling**: Workers will need to adapt to the changing job landscape by acquiring new skills in areas like programming, data analysis, and AI ethics. Governments and organizations will need to invest in **reskilling programs** to ensure that workers are prepared for the jobs of the future.

3. **AI and Human Collaboration**:
- ○ Instead of replacing humans, AI will enhance human capabilities, enabling workers to focus on tasks that require creativity, emotional intelligence, and complex decision-making. In fields like education, healthcare, and

266

entertainment, AI can act as a collaborator rather than a replacement, amplifying human potential.

Example: In healthcare, doctors will use AI to assist with diagnostics, but the doctor's expertise, empathy, and judgment in treatment decisions will still be crucial.

The Role of Machine Learning in Advancing Technology

Machine learning is a driving force behind the rapid advancement of technology across many industries. By enabling systems to learn from data and make predictions or decisions, ML is helping to solve complex problems and innovate in ways that were previously unimaginable.

1. **Advancements in Healthcare**:
   - **Personalized Medicine**: Machine learning algorithms are being used to tailor medical treatments based on a patient's genetic profile, lifestyle, and medical history, leading to more effective treatments and better outcomes.
   - **Drug Discovery**: ML models can analyze molecular data and predict which compounds are likely to be effective treatments for diseases, speeding up the drug discovery process.

267

- ○ **Healthcare Automation**: From robotic surgery to AI-powered diagnostic tools, machine learning is automating many aspects of healthcare, improving efficiency, reducing errors, and enhancing patient care.

2. **Advancements in Autonomous Systems**:

- ○ **Self-Driving Cars**: Machine learning is essential in enabling autonomous vehicles to interpret their environment, make decisions in real-time, and navigate safely.
- ○ **Robotics**: Machine learning is also improving the capabilities of robots, allowing them to perform complex tasks in manufacturing, delivery, and even healthcare (e.g., robot-assisted surgeries).

3. **Advancements in Natural Language Processing**:

- ○ **Language Translation**: Machine learning is enabling more accurate and fluent language translation systems, such as Google Translate, by learning from vast amounts of multilingual data.
- ○ **AI-Powered Virtual Assistants**: Virtual assistants like Siri, Alexa, and Google Assistant use machine learning to understand and respond to user queries, improving over time based on user interactions.
- ○ **Text Generation**: Models like GPT-3 are pushing the boundaries of natural language

understanding, enabling machines to write articles, poetry, code, and even engage in conversation with humans.

4. **Advancements in Computer Vision**:

   o **Facial Recognition**: Machine learning has revolutionized facial recognition systems, enabling applications from security to personalized experiences in retail and social media.

   o **Medical Imaging**: ML is being used to analyze medical images (e.g., CT scans, MRIs) for faster and more accurate diagnoses, aiding healthcare professionals in identifying conditions such as cancer and heart disease.

5. **Advancements in Business and Consumer Experience**:

   o **Personalized Recommendations**: ML algorithms are the backbone of recommendation systems used by companies like Netflix, Amazon, and Spotify to personalize content and product suggestions based on user behavior and preferences.

   o **Customer Support**: AI-powered chatbots and virtual assistants use ML to handle customer inquiries, improving response times and customer satisfaction.

Key Takeaways:

- **Emerging Trends**: **Federated learning, quantum computing**, and **AI ethics** are shaping the future of machine learning and AI, with potential benefits in privacy, computational power, and fairness.
- **AI's Impact on Jobs**: While AI will automate many tasks, it will also create new job opportunities and transform existing roles, emphasizing the need for reskilling and upskilling.
- **Advancements in Technology**: Machine learning is driving innovation across healthcare, autonomous systems, natural language processing, computer vision, and business applications, providing more efficient solutions and enhancing human capabilities.

In the next chapter, we will explore **Ethical and Responsible AI Development**, focusing on ensuring that AI technologies are developed and deployed in a way that benefits society and adheres to ethical principles.

CHAPTER 27

CONCLUSION AND NEXT STEPS

Recap of Key Concepts and Takeaways

Throughout this book, we've explored the fundamentals and advanced topics in machine learning (ML), covering a wide range of techniques, models, and applications. Here's a brief recap of the key concepts and takeaways from the chapters:

1. **Introduction to Machine Learning**: We started by understanding what machine learning is, the different types (supervised, unsupervised, and reinforcement learning), and the essential role of data in building ML models.

2. **Data Preprocessing**: We discussed the importance of clean, well-prepared data. Preprocessing steps like handling missing values, normalizing data, and encoding features are crucial for building effective models.

3. **Supervised Learning**: We learned about supervised learning algorithms like regression and classification models, and how they can be used to make predictions based on labeled data.

4. **Unsupervised Learning**: We explored unsupervised learning techniques like clustering and dimensionality

271

reduction, used to uncover patterns in data without predefined labels.

5. **Deep Learning**: We dove into deep learning, including neural networks, CNNs, and RNNs, which are used for tasks like image recognition, natural language processing, and time-series forecasting.

6. **Model Evaluation and Tuning**: We highlighted the importance of evaluating model performance using metrics like accuracy, precision, recall, and F1 score, as well as techniques for improving models like cross-validation, regularization, and hyperparameter tuning.

7. **Advanced Topics**: We explored cutting-edge technologies like **GANs** for generating data, **reinforcement learning** for decision-making in dynamic environments, and **explainable AI (XAI)** for making models more interpretable.

8. **Ethical Considerations**: We also covered the ethical implications of machine learning, including bias in models, fairness, privacy concerns, and transparency in decision-making systems.

9. **Industry Applications**: Machine learning is revolutionizing industries like healthcare, finance, and retail. We looked at how ML is used for disease prediction, fraud detection, personalized recommendations, and more.

10. **Future Trends**: Finally, we explored emerging trends like **federated learning**, **quantum computing**, and the evolving ethical landscape of AI, which will shape the future of ML.

Building Your First Real-World Machine Learning Application

After gaining an understanding of the core principles and techniques of machine learning, it's time to put your knowledge into practice. Building a real-world ML application can be a rewarding and challenging experience. Here's a general roadmap for building your first ML application:

1. **Define the Problem**:
   o Identify the real-world problem you want to solve. For example, you could focus on predicting stock prices, classifying emails as spam or not, or building a recommendation system.
   o Understand the business requirements, success metrics, and constraints of the project.

2. **Data Collection**:
   o Gather and clean the data you'll need to train your model. You can use publicly available datasets (e.g., Kaggle, UCI Machine Learning

273

Repository) or collect your own data from sensors, APIs, or web scraping.

- o Ensure that the data is relevant, representative, and properly formatted for the task at hand.

3. **Data Preprocessing**:

- o Perform essential preprocessing steps like cleaning, normalizing, and feature engineering to prepare the data for modeling.
- o Handle missing values, remove outliers, and encode categorical variables as needed.

4. **Model Selection**:

- o Choose an appropriate model based on the task. For example:
  - **Supervised learning**: Linear regression, decision trees, or neural networks for classification or regression tasks.
  - **Unsupervised learning**: K-means clustering or DBSCAN for customer segmentation or anomaly detection.
- o If you're new to machine learning, start with simpler models like linear regression or decision trees before progressing to more complex models like deep learning.

5. **Model Training**:

o   Split your data into training and testing sets. Use the training set to train your model and the test set to evaluate its performance.

o   Use metrics like accuracy, F1 score, or mean squared error (MSE) to assess how well the model is performing.

6. **Model Evaluation and Improvement**:

o   After training the model, evaluate it on unseen data to check its ability to generalize.

o   If the model isn't performing well, consider tuning hyperparameters, adding more data, or using advanced techniques like cross-validation or regularization.

7. **Deployment**:

o   Once you have a model that performs well, deploy it as an API using frameworks like **Flask** or **Django** to serve predictions.

o   If deploying at scale, consider using cloud platforms like **AWS**, **Google Cloud**, or **Azure** to manage deployment and scaling.

8. **Monitoring and Maintenance**:

o   After deployment, continuously monitor the model's performance to ensure it remains accurate over time. Retrain the model periodically with updated data to account for changing patterns.

Next Steps: Continuing Your Machine Learning Journey

Machine learning is a rapidly evolving field with new techniques, tools, and applications emerging regularly. Here are some steps you can take to continue your learning journey:

1. **Advanced Courses**:
   - Enroll in specialized online courses and certifications in advanced machine learning topics such as deep learning, reinforcement learning, or natural language processing. Websites like **Coursera, edX, Udacity**, and **Kaggle** offer a wealth of learning resources.

2. **Project-Based Learning**:
   - The best way to deepen your understanding is through hands-on projects. Work on personal projects or contribute to open-source ML projects. Use platforms like **GitHub** to share your work and learn from others.

3. **Research Papers and Journals**:
   - Stay updated on the latest advancements in the field by reading research papers from top conferences like **NeurIPS, ICML**, and **CVPR**. Understanding cutting-edge techniques will allow you to apply the latest methods to your projects.

4. **Competitions and Challenges**:

   o Participate in ML competitions on platforms like **Kaggle**. Competitions help you sharpen your skills and expose you to real-world problems that require creative solutions.

5. **Networking**:

   o Engage with the machine learning community by attending conferences, webinars, and meetups. Follow ML experts on social media and participate in discussions to stay updated and expand your professional network.

Additional Resources: Books, Courses, and Communities

1. **Books**:

   o *"Hands-On Machine Learning with Scikit-Learn, Keras, and TensorFlow"* by Aurélien Géron

   o *"Deep Learning"* by Ian Goodfellow, Yoshua Bengio, and Aaron Courville

   o *"Pattern Recognition and Machine Learning"* by Christopher M. Bishop

   o *"The Hundred-Page Machine Learning Book"* by Andriy Burkov

2. **Courses**:

- o **Coursera**: Machine Learning by Andrew Ng, Deep Learning Specialization, Applied Data Science with Python
- o **edX**: AI for Everyone by Andrew Ng, Professional Certificate in Machine Learning
- o **Udacity**: Machine Learning Engineer Nanodegree, Deep Learning Nanodegree
- o **Kaggle**: Courses on specific ML techniques and datasets

3. **Communities**:
   - o **Kaggle**: Participate in discussions, share notebooks, and explore datasets.
   - o **Stack Overflow**: Engage with the community to solve problems and share knowledge.
   - o **Reddit**: Subreddits like r/MachineLearning and r/DataScience are great places to discuss ML topics.
   - o **LinkedIn**: Connect with professionals in the AI and ML space, and participate in relevant groups.

Final Thoughts

Machine learning is a transformative field that is revolutionizing industries across the globe. By understanding its principles, techniques, and applications, you've gained the foundational knowledge to tackle real-world problems using ML. Whether you choose to specialize in deep learning, natural language processing, computer vision, or another subfield, the possibilities are endless.

The journey of learning machine learning is ongoing, and by continuing to practice, explore, and engage with the community, you'll be well-positioned to make a meaningful impact in the field.

Happy learning, and welcome to the world of machine learning!